back and forth across the Atlantic from rural Rusyn villages to the industrial centers of northeast America was quite common.

Almost without exception the immigrant ships headed for New York City, passed the Statue of Liberty, and docked along the wharves of the world's largest urban complex. Immediately, the immigrants were transferred to small ferries and taken to Ellis Island on the New Jersey side of the harbor. There, in isolation from the mainland, they were inspected primarily for potential health problems. In most, but not all, cases they received a stamp of approval, and some were even given a new name by immigration officers unsympathetic to or impatient with the strange sounding Slavic names. After passing these hurdles, they were released to find their way to waiting friends, relatives, or prospective employers.

As might be expected, the Carpatho-Rusyn newcomers were, in the main, members of the working class. According to United States statistics for the years 1900 through 1914, of the 254,000 "Ruthenians" who came from Austria-Hungary during those years, 41 percent were engaged in agriculture, 22 percent were laborers, and 20 percent were domestic servants. Only 2 percent were skilled artisans, less than 1 percent professionals, and even fewer were merchants. To complete the demographic picture, 13 percent were women and children without occupational status. During these years, 71 percent of "Ruthenian" immigrants were males, and only 33 percent of the total population over 14 years of age were literate.

While these figures may give us some idea of the socioeconomic character of the immigration, it is difficult, if not impossible, to determine the exact number of Carpatho-Rusyns who came to the United States. Official reports are not much help. Nonetheless, by extrapolating from various sources, it is reasonable to say that before 1914 approximately 225,000 Carpatho-Rusyns emigrated to the United States. While a few individuals had begun to arrive as early as the 1860s, it was not until the late 1880s and 1890s that substantial numbers came, the movement reaching its height during the first decade of the twentieth century.

This pre-World War I influx of Carpatho-Rusyns was not to be repeated. The war years (1914-1918) put a virtual halt to all emigration. Then, after 1920, when the political situation stabi-

lized and Carpatho-Rusyns found themselves within two new states—Czechoslovakia and Poland—migration resumed. The composition of these immigrants differed at least initially from the pre-1914 group in that women and children now predominated, as they joined husbands and fathers who had already left before the war. Before long, however, there were new impediments to what had become the somewhat common bidirectional movement of people between east-central Europe and America. This time the restrictions were imposed by the United States, which enacted in 1924 a national quota system that was highly unfavorable to the further entry of immigrants from eastern and southern Europe. Therefore, as a result of the 1924 quota system and world economic depression in the 1930s, which reduced further the ability to find the means to travel and the possibility of finding jobs, only 8,000 Carpatho-Rusyns left Czechoslovakia for the United States and 10,000 from Poland between 1920 and 1938. Faced with the American restrictions, many Carpatho-Rusyns from Czechoslovakia went instead

5. Slavic immigrant awaiting processing at Ellis Island, *ca.* 1908 (photo by Lewis Hine).

THE PROBLEM OF STATISTICS

It is impossible to know the number of Americans of Carpatho-Rusyn background in the United States. Among the reasons for this lack of information are: (1) inadequate or non-existent statistical data, whether from sending countries or from the United States; and (2) the decision of many of the first-generation immigrants and their descendants not to identify themselves as Rusyns. The latter problem is typical for many peoples who do not have their own states.

Most often, when traveling or living abroad, "stateless peoples" identify with the country in which they were born, even if their own nationality or ethnocultural background may be different from the dominant one in their home country. Thus, numerous immigrants from the pre-World War I Austro-Hungarian or Russian Empires identified—or were identified by others—as Austrians, Hungarians, or Russians, even though ethnically they were not Austrian, Hungarian, or Russian.

There is also the question of what is meant by the term Rusyn American. Does this refer to a person of Carpatho-Rusyn background who has immigrated to the United States, or can it refer as well to the offspring of such a person? If the latter, do both parents or grandparents have to be of Carpatho-Rusyn background, or is one ancestor sufficient? For our purposes, a Rusyn American is defined as any person born in the European homeland or born in the United States of at least one parent, grandparent, or other generational ancestor who came from one of the 1,022 Rusyn villages listed in the Root Seeker's appendix to this volume or, if born elsewhere (in a nearby town), someone who chooses to self-identify as a Rusyn.

Why are official or governmental statistics not helpful? First of all, it was not until as recently as 1980 that the United States Census Bureau recognized the name Rusyn, although it was to be still another decade—the census of 1990—before the census data actually indicated Americans who identified themselves as Carpatho-Rusyns. Prior to 1990, Rusyns were classified in many other ways.

Between 1899 and 1914, which coincides with the heaviest period of Carpatho-Rusyn immigration, United States statistics reported the arrival of 254,000 Ruthenians/Russniaks. Since there was an average annual return migration of 16.7 percent, this left 212,000 Ruthenians in the United States.

That figure needs to be revised, however. First of all, the terms *Ruthenian/Russniak* are not entirely helpful, because many Ukrainians—at least before 1914—also identified themselves as Ruthenians. Nonetheless, informed observers suggest that during the pre-World War I period, at least 60 percent of immigrants classified as *Ruthenians/Russniaks* were from Carpatho-Rusyn inhabited villages in northeastern Hungary and the Lemko Region of Galicia. Therefore, between 1899 and 1914, at least 152,000 immigrants classified as Ruthenians/Russniaks arrived in the United States from the Carpatho-Rusyn homeland. We also know from the 1910, 1920, and 1930 U.S. census reports that an average of 32 percent of Carpatho-Rusyn immigrants from Hungary (and later Czechoslovakia) described themselves as "Russians." This means another 73,000 must be added for a total of 225,000.

Yet even this figure has its limitations, because it does not include immigration before 1899 nor those Rusyns who chose to identify—or who were identified by others—as Austrians, Hungarians, Poles, Slovaks, or simply as "Slavish." We know from other sources that the use of the name "Slavish" was particularly widespread. Nonetheless, by reworking official United States data, it can be concluded that before World War I at least 225,000 Carpatho-Rusyns immigrated to the United States.

Statistics from the sending countries have some value but limitations as well. For instance, Hungarian records indicated that 55,000 Rusyns left Hungary between 1889 and 1913; while official and unofficial sources suggest that for the longer period between 1880 and 1913 as many as 62,000 emigrated. Since 97 percent of Hungary's Rusyn emigrants went to the United States, the corrected figure would be 60,000.

The problem with these statistics is that they record only legal departures. Records from German ports, the preferred route for departure, show that only half of the immigrants who passed through those ports had left Hungary legally. Thus, it is reasonable to assume that there were twice as many Carpatho-Rusyns—120,000—who emigrated to the United States from Hungary alone before World War I. In the absence of equivalent emigration statistics specifically from Rusyn villages in the Lemko Region of Galicia, we can only provide a rough estimate. Since Lemko Region villages comprise 31 percent of the total number of Carpatho-Rusyn inhabited villages, this would suggest that perhaps 55,000 Lemkos left for the United States before World War I.

Based on such limited data from the United States and the sending countries, it is reasonable to assume that during the height of immigration from East Central Europe between the years 1880 and 1914, no less than 225,000 Carpatho-Rusyns immigrated to the United States. Subsequent immigration was on a much smaller scale, consisting of about 18,000 newcomers from Czechoslovakia and Poland during the interwar years and another 7,500 from those two countries and the Soviet Ukraine in the nearly half century after World War II.

Despite such immigration figures totalling over 250,000 for the period both before and after World War I, not to mention natural demographic growth rates that by the 1990s should have produced through offspring about two and one-half times the number of original immigrants, the present figures of Carpatho-Rusyns are wholly inadequate. In 1980, the United States Census Bureau recorded only 8,485 *Ruthenians* (persons who answered Rusyn were classified as Russian), and in 1990 it recorded a total of 12,946 persons who classified themselves in five categories: *Carpatho-Rusyn* (7,316), *Ruthenian* (3,776), *Rusyn* (1,357), *Carpathian* (266), and *Lemko* (231). It is also likely that many Americans of Carpatho-Rusyn background are among the 315,285 persons who described themselves as *Czechoslovakian*, or the 122,469 *Eastern Europeans*, or the 70,552 *Slavics/Slavish*.

How, then, is it possible to obtain a more realistic estimate of the number of Americans today of Carpatho-Rusyn background? We may begin with the conservative estimate of 225,000 immigrants for the pre-1914 period. To this must be added the post-World War I immigration—primarily in the 1920s—of 8,000 from Czechoslovakia and 10,000 from the Lemko Region of what was then Poland. (Because of the world economic crisis of the 1930s and changing goals among immigrants no more than a few hundred returned home). This gives us 243,000.

Since the general population growth in the United States between 1930 and 1990 was 2½ fold, the pre-1930 first-generation immigrants and their descendants should number today around 607,000. To these must be added several smaller waves of new arrivals that came after World War II: 4,000 who came in the wake of the war before 1950; 1,000 following the crisis in Czechoslovakia in 1968; and 2,000 in the course of political changes in Poland during the 1980s. Together with their descendants, the post-World War II group includes about 15,000, leaving a total of 622,000 Carpatho-Rusyns. It is interesting to note that the estimated Carpatho-Rusyn church membership in 1991 is 596,000. Thus, while it is impossible to know the precise number of Americans of Carpatho-Rusyn background, a reasonable estimate would place the figure in 1990 somewhere between 600,000 and 625,000.

SOURCES: *13th, 14th and 15th Census of the United States* (Washington, D.C., 1913-33); Oleksander Mytsiuk, "Z emihratsiï uhro-rusyniv pered svitovoiu viinoiu," *Naukovyi zbirnyk tovarystva 'Prosvita',* XIII-XIV (Užhorod, 1938), pp. 21-32; Wasyl Halich, *Ukrainians in the United States* (Chicago, 1937), esp. pp. 150-153; Julianna Puskás, *From Hungary to the United States, 1880-1914* (Budapest, 1982); Julianna Puskás, ed., *Overseas Migration from East-Central and South-Eastern Europe, 1880-1940* (Budapest, 1990), esp. pp. 46-58.

(generally as sojourning workers who planned to return home after a few years) to Argentina or Uruguay, while about 10,000 from the Lemko Region—in what was by then Poland— went to settle permanently in Canada.

World War II interrupted the normal if limited flow of people, but it did lead to the phenomenon of displaced persons who for political reasons were unable or unwilling to return to their homeland. About 4,000 of these "DPs" were Carpatho-Rusyns who, between 1945 and 1950, eventually found their way, often via displaced persons' camps in Germany and Austria, to the United States or Canada. By 1950, the Soviet Union and the east-central European countries under its political control effectively barred emigration from the Carpatho-Rusyn homeland for most of the four decades

of Communist rule that lasted until 1989-1991. The exceptions were the periods of political liberalization in Czechoslovakia (1968) and Poland (1980-1981), which produced in their wake the arrival of about 3,000 new Carpatho-Rusyn immigrants in the United States and Canada.

Because of the lack of reliable statistics from Europe, the specific character of United States statistics, and the tendency of many immigrants to describe themselves in a manner other than Carpatho-Rusyn, we cannot know with any certainty the number of Carpatho-Rusyn Americans. Nonetheless, estimates based on United States census data, on statistics from sending countries, and on membership in churches suggest that by the early 1990s there were at least 600,000 Carpatho-Rusyns and their descendants in the United States.

Carpatho-Rusyn Church Statistics in the United States

Church	Membership 1991	Carpatho-Rusyn Membership (estimate)
Byzantine Ruthenian Catholic Metropolitan Archdiocese	244,000	195,000
American Carpatho-Russian Orthodox Greek Catholic Church	20,000	18,000
Orthodox Church in America	1,000,000[*]	250,000
Russian Orthodox Church in the U.S.A.—the Patriarchal Parishes	10,000 (1985 figure)	8,000
Other Orthodox, Ukrainian Catholic, Roman Catholic, and Protestant denominations	—	125,000
Total		596,000

[*]Many suggest this figure is inflated, that a more accurate estimate is 300,000-350,000, and that correspondingly the Carpatho-Rusyn membership is about 100,000.

SOURCE: *Official Catholic Directory for 1991* (Wilmette, Ill., 1991); *Yearbook of American and Canadian Churches* (Nashville, Tenn., 1991).

Chapter 3

Settlement Patterns and Economic Life

The initial and subsequent geographical distribution of Carpatho-Rusyn immigrants in the United States reflects their socioeconomic background, their goals, and the needs of American society in the decades before World War I, a time when the vast majority arrived. The newcomers were for the most part poor peasants, 65 percent of whom arrived before 1914 with less than $30 in money and belongings. With meagre financial resources, they were in no position to buy the relatively expensive land in the northeastern states near the port of their arrival—Ellis Island in New York City's harbor—nor to travel long distances by train to the west where cheap land was still available.

In any case, most did not plan to make the United States their permanent home. Their stay was to be merely for a few years, or as long as it took to earn enough money in order to return home and buy that all-important peasant commodity—land. Because most were temporary sojourners, they were interested in finding whatever jobs would pay the most. As for American society, it was going through a period of rapid industrial expansion, especially in the northeast, and was therefore in need of a large, unskilled industrial work force to man its mines and factories. Thus, the needs of American industry and the desires of Carpatho-Rusyn immigrants complemented each other.

Carpatho-Rusyn newcomers settled for the most part in the northeast. The first center to attract them during the 1880s and 1890s was the coal-mining belt in eastern Pennsylvania, near Scranton and Wilkes-Barre, and in smaller coal towns like Hazleton, Freeland, Mahanoy City, and Olyphant. The industrial plants of New York City and its suburb Yonkers, as well as the southern Connecticut city of Bridgeport and the northern New Jersey factories and oil refineries in Passaic, Bayonne, Elizabeth, Rahway, Perth Amboy, and Manville also attracted Carpatho-Rusyn immigrants in search of work. But by the outset of the twentieth century, the newest center of settlement became western Pennsylvania, most especially Pittsburgh and its suburbs like Homestead, Munhall, McKeesport, McKees Rocks, Monessen, Braddock, Clairton, and Duquesne. In these places, as well as in Johnstown about 75 miles to the east, it was the steel mills and related industries that provided jobs for Rusyns and other immigrants of Slavic background.

Soon concentrations of Carpatho-Rusyns were also found in the industrial centers of nearby states: Binghamton, Endicott, and Johnson City in south-central New York; Cleveland, Parma, and Youngstown in Ohio; Gary and Whiting in Indiana; Chicago and Joliet in Illinois; Detroit and Flint in Michigan; and Minneapolis in Minnesota. It is not surprising, therefore, that in the period 1910-1920, as high as 79 percent of the Carpatho-Rusyns lived in the urban areas of the Middle Atlantic states. This included 54 percent in Pennsylvania, 13 percent in New York, and 12 percent in New Jersey, followed by Ohio, Connecticut, and Illinois. Despite this basic settlement pattern centered in the northeast industrial belt, it is nonetheless interesting to note that some Carpatho-Rusyns

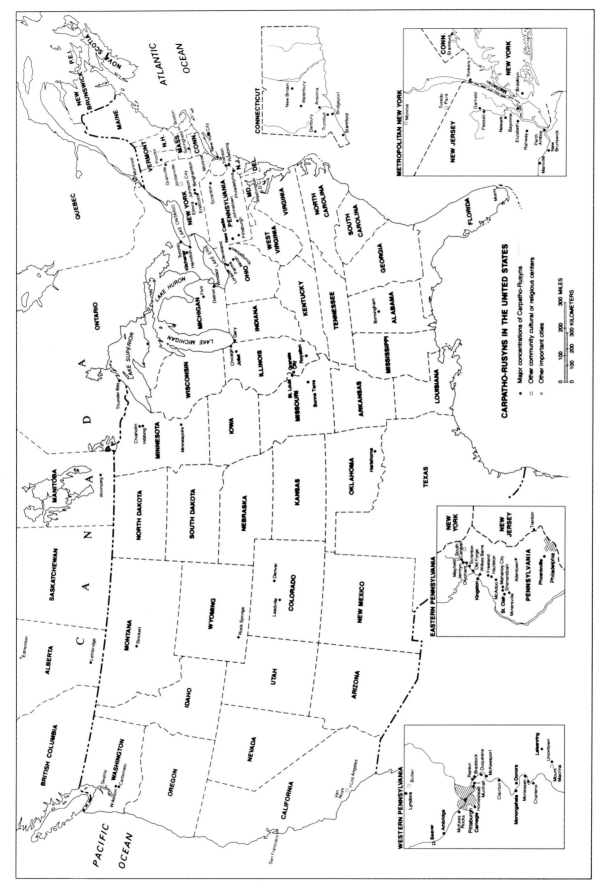

CARPATHO-RUSYNS IN THE UNITED STATES

- Major concentrations of Carpatho-Rusyns
- Other community cultural or religious centers
- Other important cities

MAP 4

6. Workers on their way to the coal mines in Lattimore, Pennsylvania, *ca.* 1900 (photo by Rise and Gates).

ventured to a few out-of-the-way and unexpected places. Thus, the marble industry attracted a small group who established a community in Proctor, Vermont, while some went south to start farms in Virginia or to work in the steel mills of Birmingham, Alabama. In the mid-west, Carpatho-Rusyns were drawn to the coal mines around Royalton in southern Illinois; to the varied industries of St. Louis, Missouri and the steel mills of nearby Granite City, Illinois; to the lead mines around Bonne Terre and Desloge, Missouri; to the coal mines near Hartshorne and Haileyville, Oklahoma; and farther north to the iron mines of Chisholm and Hibbing in upstate Minnesota. Some even ventured as far west as the gold, silver, and lead mines in Leadville, Colorado; the railroad in Rock Springs, Wyoming; the copper mines in Stockett, Montana; and the coal mining settlements of Carbonado and Wilkeson in the Carbon River valley just south of Seattle, Washington.

In view of the temporary nature of their intended stay in the New World, Carpatho-Rusyns often moved into company-owned houses and tenements near the mines or factories where they worked. A high percentage of single males (which characterized the group before World War I) lived in boardinghouses often supervised by the wife of a Carpatho-Rusyn or fellow Slavic immigrant. While these early living quarters were often overcrowded and polluted with industrial smoke and noise—a far cry from the placid rural environment of the Carpathian mountain homeland—they nonetheless did provide a certain degree of psychological security in an otherwise strange land in that the majority of their neighbors were Rusyns or other Slavic and eastern European immigrants.

By the 1920s, political conditions in Europe (including the upheaval of World War I that had cut off migration across the Atlantic) as well as adaptation to American life (enhanced by a gradual increase in monetary savings and the establishment of family life through marriages in the New World or the arrival of wives and children from the Old) were factors which convinced many Carpatho-Rusyns that their temporary work visits might preferably become permanent. When by the 1950s, Carpatho-Rusyns had become psychologically as well as physically established in America, some first-generation immigrants, and certainly their second- and third-generation descendants, began to move out of the company-owned houses and inner-city tenements to the surrounding suburbs. With the decline of American inner cities, especially during the 1970s, the traditional "Carpatho-Rusyn ghettos" all but disappeared in the downtown areas of big cities like New York, Passaic, Pittsburgh, and Cleveland. The churches do remain, however, and are attended mainly by parishioners who arrive in cars to spend a few hours each Sunday morning before returning to their suburban homes.

While the desire to remain in or near one's original birthplace in the northeastern United States continued to be strong, by the 1970s a new trend had developed. Following general demographic and settlement patterns in the United States, Carpatho-Rusyns began moving to the sunbelt states of Florida, California, and Arizona. Those who have chosen this route include the original first-generation immigrants and their now elderly second-generation offspring who fear the dangers of urban life in the northeast and who, at their advanced age, prefer the warmer climates of the south and west, as well as second-, third-, and fourth-generation professionals who are forced to

move at the behest of their employers.

Nonetheless, despite these relatively recent developments, the majority of the Carpatho-Rusyns as well as their religious and secular organizations remain within the industrial cities of the northeastern and north-central states. For instance, of the 296 parishes in the Byzantine Ruthenian Catholic Church and the American Carpatho-Russian Orthodox Greek Catholic Church, 80 percent are still located in four states: Pennsylvania (50 percent), Ohio (13 percent), New Jersey (11 percent), and New York (6 percent).

Since the vast majority of Carpatho-Rusyns who arrived in the United States were poor peasants, it is not surprising that, with few exceptions, they were forced to seek their livelihood among the ranks of unskilled laborers. Thus, the first generation found employment in the factories, mines, and steel mills of the northeast United States. In the coal industry, where many obtained their first jobs, they began as miner's helpers usually receiving no more than a third of the miner's normal

7. Women, including many Carpatho-Rusyns, on the assembly line at the Endicott-Johnson Shoe Company Jigger Factory, Johnson City, New York, *ca.* 1930.

wage, while in factories and steel mills they were first hired to do the most menial tasks. Gradually, they moved up to become miners or semi-skilled and skilled factory laborers in their own right. Because they generally were at the lowest end of the working man's income level, it was not surprising to find Carpatho-Rusyns taking part in the many strikes that rocked the industrial and coal mining regions of Pennsylvania and neighboring states, especially in the decades before World War I. Still, it must be admitted that because Rusyn workers were primarily concerned with earning quick cash in order to return to the European homeland, they were likely to accept harsher work conditions and to avoid strike and anti-company activity which might jeopardize their goals.

Carpatho-Rusyn women, who began to come in larger numbers just before and after World War I, often found employment—especially if they were single—as servants or maids in the households of wealthy Americans or even the increasing number of well-to-do eastern European Jews and Slavs. As they became more adjusted to the American environment, Carpatho-Rusyn women began to work as waitresses or retail salespersons and in light industries such as shoe, soap, and cigar factories, or in laundries and garment works. Those women who were already or who became married were expected to remain at home and care for the children and household. Besides these onerous tasks, however, they often had to supplement their husband's income—especially in times of economic hardship or strikes—by hiring themselves out as domestics or by working part-time in stores or mills.

There were, of course, among Carpatho-Rusyns, a small percentage of more ambitious individuals who from the earliest years of the immigration tried their luck at founding and operating small businesses. Among the most popular outlets were enterprises that served the needs of their fellow immigrants, such as butcher shops, groceries, taverns, and small restaurants. Some even entered the ranks of white-collar businessmen, as operators of funeral homes, travel and package-sending agencies, or as editors and officials in community organizations, most especially the fraternals. Women also expanded their economic potential by turning their residences into boarding-houses, where they provided rooms and cooked meals for single male workers.

As individuals whose original peasant mentality placed great importance on acquiring material security and a modicum of wealth, Carpatho-Rusyns could accept quite easily the American mainstream ideology which promised rewards for those who worked hard and lived a "decent," even frugal life. The same peasant mentality also contained, however, an undisciplined come-what-may attitude, which sometimes led to an unending cycle of hard work (according to the merciless clock of modern industry and not the more humane "sun clock" of nature) followed by "relief" in heavy drinking. Not surprisingly, frequent and often daily visits to the local tavern (korčma) on the way home from work would cut deeply into whatever savings had been acquired. Alcoholism, then, especially in the early years, became a problem for many Carpatho-Rusyn workers, although they soon learned that if they wanted to improve their financial status they would have to become more disciplined and to give up the tradition of less structured work and living habits.

It seems that the American environment and the attraction of potentially improved living circumstances proved to be the stronger force. Even in the early years, official United States statistics (1904-1905) reported that along with Bulgarians and other South Slavic immigrants, "Ruthenians" had the lowest proportion (.04 percent) of people in public charities and, for that matter, in penal institutions. Subsequently, the few statistics that are available show a distinct rise in the economic status of Carpatho-Rusyns. By the second generation, that is, among the American-born who began their working careers after World War I, the majority of Carpatho-Rusyns had become skilled and semi-skilled workers, foremen, or clerical workers. By the third generation, there was a marked increase in managerial and semi-professional occupations.

Nonetheless, it seems that the socioeconomic structure of third- and fourth-generation Carpatho-Rusyns is not as oriented toward upward social mobility as that of other groups—Jews, Italians, Greeks, Hungarians—whose parents and grandparents also arrived in large numbers at the outset of the twentieth century. To be sure, there were a few large companies founded by Carpatho-Rusyns who became wealthy through business skills, such

8. Coal miner families relaxing on a Sunday afternoon in eastern Pennsylvania, *ca.* 1900.

as the Peerless Aluminum Foundry in Bridgeport, Connecticut of the Peter Hardy family, the Manhattan Building Supply in New York City of the Mahonec family, and the Liberty Tool Corporation in Bridgeport, Connecticut of John Cipkala. There was even a Hungaro-Russian Slavonic State Bank that operated during the first decades of this century in Johnstown, Pennsylvania under the direction of George Kondor.

Particularly successful in the business world was the son of Lemko immigrants to Canada and later the New York investor, Paul M. Fekula. Raised in the Orthodox religious tradition, Fekula was embued with a Russian identity and Pan-Slavic spirit which led him to amass the largest private collection of Slavic books and old manuscripts in North America. But by far the most successful private entrepreneur was Stephen B. Roman, a native of the Prešov Region in Slovakia and a self-professed "Rusnak Slovak." Roman was one of the earliest developers of uranium mining in Canada.

He founded and until his death in the late 1980s headed Denison Mines Limited, a multimillion dollar conglomerate based in Toronto, Ontario, with several subsidiary companies in oil, gas, coal, potash, and banking located in Canada and other countries. Despite his business interests, Roman was a fervent community activist, especially instrumental in the creation in 1982 of the Slovak Byzantine-rite Catholic Diocese of Canada.

The Carpatho-Rusyn immigration has also produced a small but steadily increasing number of professionals—lawyers, physicians, dentists, university professors, and, in particular, school teachers and nurses—most of whom are from the second, third, and fourth generation. Nonetheless, the ultimate goal for most Rusyns is to attain a place in "middle-class" America and to be satisfied with working for an established company which provides limited advancement but a measure of financial security that will permit the ownership of one's own home and a modest bank account.

Chapter 4

Religious Life

Another part of the cultural traditions or collective psyche that Carpatho-Rusyns brought to America was their attitude toward religion. Religion, in the form of Eastern Christianity, had always been an integral part of Carpatho-Rusyn community life, at least until the advent of Communist-dominated governments in their homeland after 1945. The whole village life-cycle used to be governed by the church. The traditional peasant mode of existence, determined by the climatic changes of the agricultural seasons, was interspersed by numerous religious holidays, including workless Sundays, fasts and feasts of the church calendar, baptisms, marriages, and funerals—all carried out according to the fixed guidelines of the church. Since religious life was so bound up with the Carpatho-Rusyn mentality, it was only natural that the first immigrants attempted to recreate for themselves a similar environment in the United States. In this they were quite successful, so that even after three, four, and five generations, Carpatho-Rusyn community life in the United States continues to rely almost exclusively on an individual's relation to the church.

In essence, the history of Carpatho-Rusyns in the United States is virtually synonymous with the group's religious development. And this development has been the story of the successes and failures of the Greek (later known as the Byzantine Ruthenian) Catholic Church in its attempts to maintain its traditional rights and privileges in the

face of encroachments by the dominant Roman Catholic hierarchy. Nonetheless, at various times the Greek (Byzantine Ruthenian) Catholic Church has had to forfeit certain traditions. This has led to rebellion on the part of many Carpatho-Rusyn priests and parishioners, who consequently left their original church and either joined existing religious bodies, especially various Orthodox churches, or set up new ones.

The organizational history of the Greek Catholic Church began with the establishment of its very first parishes, including three in eastern Pennsylvania—Shenandoah (1884), Freeland (1886), Hazleton (1887)—and one in Minneapolis, Minnesota (1887). For nearly three decades, these and other early parishes included Greek Catholics not only from the Hungarian Kingdom (Carpatho-Rusyns as well as Slovaks and some Magyars), but also those from north of the Carpathian Mountains in Austrian Galicia, including Rusyns who called themselves Lemkos and those who after living in America began to identify themselves as Ukrainians or as Russians.

It was the people themselves who took the initiative to organize parishes, build churches, and request priests from Europe. The very first Greek Catholic priest to arrive in America was Father John Volansky, who in 1884 came to Shenandoah, Pennsylvania. He was followed by Zenon Liakhovych and Constantine Andrukhovych, both of whom were also from Galicia. The next priest to

9. St. Mary's Greek Catholic Church, Freeland, Pennsylvania, built 1887. This is the original church of the oldest parish still within the Byzantine Ruthenian Catholic Church.

10. One of the earliest group photographs in the United States of Byzantine Rite (Greek) Catholic priests, Wilkes Barre, Pennsylvania, 1890. Seated left to right: Gabriel Vislocky, Ivan Zapotocky, Alexis Toth, Theofan Obushkevich; standing left to right: Eugene Volkay, Alexander Dzubay, Stefan Jackovics, Gregory Hrushka.

arrive, in 1889, was Father Alexander Dzubay, who was the first to come from Rusyn lands south of the Carpathians in Hungary. From then on, the majority of priests came from Hungary, so that by 1894, out of more than 20 Greek Catholic priests, only 4 were from Galicia.

These early priests arrived in an environment that was not hospitable to Greek (Byzantine-rite) Catholicism. Volansky, for instance, was not recognized by the Latin-rite Archbishop of Philadelphia, Patrick J. Ryan, who forbade him to perform his priestly functions. Not only was the Irish-dominated Roman Catholic hierarchy unsympathetic, but fellow Slavic Catholic priests, especially Poles, also scorned these seemingly strange Eastern-rite Catholics.

The main reason for the generally cold reception was the ignorance that prevailed among American Catholic leaders about anything other than the Latin rite within their own "universal" church. Another factor was the trend in certain Catholic circles and public life in general known as Americanization. There was even a National Americanization Committee, which was engaged in an effort to make the foreign-born "give up the languages, customs, and methods of life which they have brought with them across the ocean, and to adopt instead the language, habits, and customs of this country, and the general standards and ways of American living."[1] And if the habits of immigrants from the old country might be difficult to change, then for sure their American-born or acculturized children must become fully assimilated. The best way to achieve that goal and the process of Americanization in general was through the school system, which should instill "an appreciation of the institutions of this country and absolute forgetfulness of all obligations or connections with other countries, because of descent or birth."[2]

In this connection, it should be remembered that the Catholic Church in the United States had, since colonial days, experienced varying kinds of

discrimination and lingering social intolerance, the kind of intolerance encountered by all religious groups that did not belong to mainstream Protestantism. Although the Roman Catholic Church officially condemned Americanization, a few Catholic leaders welcomed certain aspects of it in the hope that their church would finally be accepted fully into American society. Hence, in an attempt to prove their "Americanness," Catholic leaders headed by Bishop Ryan in Philadelphia and Bishop John Ireland in St. Paul, Minnesota were anxious to remove all ethnic distinctions within the Roman Catholic Church. The church was simply to became an American institution and an instrument of assimilation. Through such a "progressive" policy, these Catholic leaders hoped finally to have Catholicism fully accepted in American life.

It was into such an environment that Greek or Byzantine-rite Catholics arrived. While it is true that the ethnic Poles or Slovaks—even the "racially" more acceptable Germans—may have used their native languages and still have followed certain Old-World religious practices, they at least were of the Latin rite. The Carpatho-Rusyns, on the other hand, were of the Byzantine rite; therefore, they used Church Slavonic instead of Latin in their liturgies and they observed the Julian calendar (about two weeks later) instead of the "normal" Gregorian calendar. And as if that was not bad enough, their priests could be married. This seemed nothing less than the ultimate anathema! Not surprisingly, therefore, Bishop Ryan's rejection of Father Volansky was repeated time and again toward other Greek Catholic priests. They were often forbidden to issue the sacraments, to bury their parishioners in Roman Catholic cemetaries, and they were snubbed by the Roman Catholic clergy in the communities where they lived.

Left to its own devices, the community and its few priests took matters into their own hands. Often led by Carpatho-Rusyn businessmen, parishes bought property and built their own churches, which might include a meeting hall and school below the sanctuary or in a separate building. Because of the initiative of laymen in organizing church life, these early years set a pattern whereby secular leaders felt they had the right as well as obligation to be concerned with the religious developments of the community. For

[1] From a leaflet published by the National Americanization Committee, cited in Milton M. Gordon, *Assimilation in American Life* (New York, 1964), p. 101.
[2] Statement in 1918 by the Superintendent of the New York Public Schools, cited in Gordon, *Assimilation*, pp. 100-101.

11. The existence of married priests was to cause great difficulties for Byzantine Rite (Greek) Catholics in America. Here the wedding of Emil Gulyassy (to the right of the bride with flowers, Lily Mihalich) before his ordination to the priesthood. Father Anthony Mhley (on the far right) was the officiating priest at Holy Ghost Greek Catholic Church, Charleroi, Pennsylvania, 1922.

12. Secular trustees were to control many of the early Rusyn-American churches. The trustees together with three priests—top row, left to right: Fathers Nicholas Szabados, Thomas Szabo, and Cornelius Laurisin of St. Michael's Church, St. Clair, Pennsylvania, ca. 1912.

instance, church property was often not registered in the name of the bishop representing a diocese (as was to become standard Catholic practice), but rather in the name of a board of lay trustees within each individual parish. The existence of this legal arrangement subsequently was to have serious consequences for the church.

It was not long before the Vatican became aware of the difficulties that had developed between the Roman and rapidly growing Greek Catholic communities in the United States. In an attempt to clarify the situation, on October 1, 1890, the Vatican issued the first decree concerning the Greek Catholic Church in America. It specified that newly arriving Greek Catholic priests were to report to, receive jurisdiction from, and remain under the authority of the local Latin-rite bishop. Moreover, all priests had to be celibate and married priests were to be recalled to Europe. As an addendum, another Vatican decree in 1895 declared that in areas where there were no Greek Catholic churches, the parishioners could become Roman Catholic.

As might be expected, many Greek Catholic priests felt that their century-old traditions dating

13. Father Alexis G. Toth.

back to the Union of Brest (1596) and Union of Užhorod (1646) were not being honored by Rome and were being directly undermined by an unsympathetic American Catholic hierarchy. Thus, already in late 1890 and again in late 1891 groups of Greek Catholic priests met and argued that their increasingly unfavorable plight would not improve until they had their own bishop. In the interim, they requested the appointment of a Carpatho-Rusyn vicar general who, in the person of Father Nicephor Chanat, was chosen to act as an intermediary between Greek Catholic priests and Latin-rite bishops.

More serious was the case of Father Alexis G. Toth. Toth was a respected seminary professor and chancellor of the Eparchy of Prešov in the Carpatho-Rusyn region of Hungary who, in 1889, was sent to the United States to serve in the parish in Minneapolis. Upon his arrival, Toth reported as expected to the local Latin-rite ordinary, Archbishop John Ireland of St. Paul. Ireland was the foremost spokesman of the Americanization movement, and because of his desire to eliminate ethnic differences, it is not surprising that he was already negatively disposed toward this new priest from east-central Europe. Because of the importance of Toth's later activity, it would be useful to quote him directly about the fateful meeting with Bishop Ireland. The following is taken from Toth's courtroom testimony delivered in 1894:

As an obedient Uniate [Greek Catholic], I complied with the orders of my Bishop, who at the time was John Valyi [of the Eparchy of Prešov], and appeared before Bishop Ireland on December 19, 1889, kissed his hand according to custom and presented my credentials, failing, however, to kneel before him, which, as I learned later, was my chief mistake. I remember that no sooner did he read that I was a 'Greek Catholic', his hands began to shake. It took him fifteen minutes to read to the end after which he asked abruptly—we conversed in Latin:
'Have you a wife?'
'No.'
'But you had one?'
'Yes, I am a widower.'
At this he threw the paper on the table and loudly exclaimed: 'I have already written to Rome protesting against this kind of priests being sent to me!'
'What kind of priests do you mean?'

'Your kind.'

'I am a Catholic priest of the Greek rite. I am a Uniate and was ordained by a regular Catholic Bishop.'

'I do not consider that either you or this bishop of yours are Catholic; besides, I do not need any Greek Catholic priests here; a Polish priest in Minneapolis is quite sufficient; the Greeks can also have him for their priest.'

'But he belongs to the Latin rite; besides our people do not understand him and so they will hardly go to him; that was the reason they instituted a church of their own.'

'They had no permission from me and I shall grant you no jurisdiction to work here.'

Deeply hurt by the fanaticism of this representative of Papal Rome, I replied sharply: 'In that case, I know the rights of my church, I know the basis on which the Union was established and shall act accordingly.'

The Archbishop lost his temper. I lost mine just as much. One word brought another, the thing had gone so far that our conversation is not worth putting on record.[3]

Despite Bishop Ireland's refusal to recognize Father Toth, the latter continued to serve his Carpatho-Rusyn parish and hope for some favorable intervention from his bishop in Europe. When no help was forthcoming, Toth felt that the centuries-old traditions of his church, recognized by Rome as canonically legal, were being violated in the New World. He therefore decided to abjure the Catholic church altogether and to convert to Orthodoxy. He travelled to San Francisco, where a Russian Orthodox bishop was residing. The result was that on March 25, 1891, Father Toth and his community of 365 Carpatho-Rusyns were formally accepted by Bishop Vladimir Sokolovsky into the Russian Orthodox Diocese of Alaska and the Aleutian Islands.

For its part, the Russian Orthodox Church was only too willing to accept Toth and his flock, for at the time Russia's tsarist government was supporting liberally the spread of Orthodoxy both in Europe and the New World. The talented Toth was before long sent on missionary work to Pennsylvania, where he succeeded in converting many more Carpatho-Rusyns to the Orthodox faith. It has been estimated that by the time of his death in 1909, this energetic priest "brought back" more than 25,000 Carpatho-Rusyns (three-quarters of whom were from the Lemko Region in Galicia) into the fold of Orthodoxy. These converts and their descendants have since then formed a significant portion of the membership in the Russian Orthodox Greek Catholic Church in America (later the "Metropolia" and now part of the Orthodox Church in America). For his work, Toth has been hailed by the church as the "father of Orthodoxy" in the United States and recently declared a saint.

Toth's proselytizing efforts did not end with his passing from the scene. They were, in fact, increased in intensity under the energetic Archbishop Platon Rozhdestvensky, who headed the Russian Orthodox Church in North America from 1907 to 1914. During his tenure, no fewer than 72 parishes or communities were received into Orthodoxy, most of them containing "Carpatho-Russian" Greek Catholics who were being urged to seek their "true home" in the Russian Orthodox Church.

In addition, Toth and Platon's missionary work was also felt beyond the borders of the New World. Some of his immigrant converts, who had returned temporarily or permanently to Europe, often brought Orthodox literature (published in

---

[3] Cited in Keith S. Russin, "Father Alexis G. Toth and the Wilkes-Barre Litigations," *St Vladimir's Theological Quarterly*, XVI, 3 (Crestwood, N.Y., 1972), pp. 132-133.

14. The original building of St. Mary's Church, Minneapolis, built 1888, the first Greek Catholic parish to join the Orthodox Church.

15. Brotherhood of the Apostles Peter and Paul, Minneapolis, founded 1891, composed of laymen from the parish of Reverend Toth (bottom center), who helped him in the struggle to join the Orthodox Church.

Russia and the United States) and dollars back to the Rusyn homeland. In fact, the first revival of Orthodoxy among Carpatho-Rusyns in east-central Europe began during the 1890s and was the result of the confluence of American immigrant dollars and Russian "rolling rubles" (funds supplied by the tsarist government) meeting in the valleys of the Carpathians.

Faced with these difficulties, the Vatican agreed in 1902 to appoint an apostolic visitor in order to study conditions among Greek Catholics in the United States. The individual chosen was Father Andrew Hodobay from the Prešov Eparchy, who after five years returned to Europe with recommendations for the appointment of a Greek Catholic bishop. From the beginning, however, Hodobay received little cooperation from Rusyn-American priests, a situation that illustrates another aspect of difficulties within the immigrant community.

Initially, all Carpatho-Rusyn and other Eastern-rite immigrants, whether from Galicia or northeastern Hungary, were united in the same Greek Catholic churches and, as we shall see, they belonged to the same fraternal organizations. But almost from the outset, regional and national differences made it impossible to maintain this arrangement. From the Carpatho-Rusyn point of view, the problem arose when young priests from Galicia (Nestor Dmytriw, John Ardan, Stephan Makar, Anton Bonchevsky and others), who were embued with Ukrainian national feeling, tried to ukrainianize their parishes. The Galician Ukrainians looked, in turn, at their fellow Carpatho-Rusyn Lemkos from Galicia as Russophiles constantly susceptible to the Orthodox "schism," and at Carpatho-Rusyns from Hungary as Magyarones who, if they did not succumb to russification, were ever ready to sell out their Slavic heritage and to magyarize their parishes. Hence, by the 1890s each newly arrived Greek Catholic priest was scrutinized by community leaders to see whether he was from Galicia or from Hungary and whether he was a Ukrainophile, a Russophile, or a Magyarone.

Because the apostolic visitor was suspected of serving the magyarizing policy of the Hungarian government, he was immediately boycotted by the Galicians (both Ukrainophile and Russophile) and later as well by many Carpatho-Rusyns (especially secular leaders) from Hungary. And if regional and national divisions were not enough, Rusyn priests were also divided along eparchial lines. This was especially prevalent among priests from Hungary, with the "aristocratic" clergy from the Mukačevo eparchy looking down on their brethren from the Prešov eparchy as being little more than uncouth "peasant types." Finally, added to the rivalries and bickering among priests was the increasingly strong influence of lay leaders, especially those associated with the first Carpatho-Rusyn fraternal organization known as the Union (Sojedinenije) of Greek Catholic Brotherhoods. Secular community leaders were well aware that they were the ones who had paid for and built the churches, rectories, and schools and who supported the priests financially. Influenced by the new American environment in which they lived, they were not about to be "subjects as it is in the Old Country . . . . to pay, support, be silent, and obey." "In the land of

Ea Semper Decree

(Excerpts from *Acta Sanctae Sedis*, Vol. XLI, Rome, 1908, pp. 3-12, trans. from Latin by Eric Csapo)

It has always been the special and proper concern of the Apostolic See that the various and diverse rites which adorn the Catholic Church be carefully preserved. Many provisions and statutes of our predecessors make clear declaration to this effect, especially as regards the venerable liturgies of the Eastern churches.

. . . . The rite of the Ruthenians could best be preserved unchanged and appropriately administered, and the Ruthenian faithful could with the approval of this council arm themselves more effectively against the dangers to which they lay exposed by the acts of schismatic citizens if a bishop were given to them. . . . We have taken counsel for the selection and nomination of a bishop who, invested with the necessary authority, will make every effort to see that the Ruthenian Greek rite be preserved unaltered in the various missions in the United States.

Article 1.   The nomination of the bishop of the Ruthenian rite for the United States is a task fully reserved for the Apostolic See.

Article 2.   The bishop of the Ruthenian rite is under the immediate jurisdiction and power of the Apostolic See and is to be overseen by the Apostolic Delegate in Washington. Moreover, he is to have no ordinary jurisdiction, but only that delegated to him by the respective bishops of the [Latin-rite] dioceses in which the Ruthenians reside.

Article 3.   The bishop of the Ruthenian rite will be able to visit his parishes provided he has the written permission of the [Latin-rite] bishop. The latter will confer such powers as he deems fit.

Article 4.   When the bishop of the Ruthenian rite visits his parishes, he will ask for an account of the property of that parish from the respective rector, and he will see that the rector does not hold in his own name and right items acquired with the help of contributions made in any way by the faithful. . . . Title to such goods shall be either transferred to the local [Latin-rite] bishop as soon as possible or be firmly assigned in any secure and legal fashion approved by the same bishop and thereby remain in support of the parish.

Article 10.   Since there are not yet any Ruthenian priests who were either born or even educated in the United States, the bishop of the Ruthenian rite, in consultation with the Apostolic Delegate and the local [Latin-rite] bishop, will make every effort to establish seminaries to educate Ruthenian priests in the United States as soon as possible. In the meantime, Ruthenian clergymen will be admitted to the Latin seminaries in the area where they were born or in which they are domiciled. But only those who are celibate at present and who shall remain so may be promoted to the sacred orders.

Article 14.   It is strictly forbidden Ruthenian priests who are resident in the United States to consign the baptized with holy chrism. If they do so despite the prohibition, they should know that their actions are invalid.

Article 17.   All rectors of Ruthenian parishes in the United States are subject to dismissal at the discretion of the local [Latin-rite] bishop. The bishop of the Ruthenian rite is to be informed in good time. No dismissal, moreover, should be ordered without serious and fair cause.

Article 21.   The Ruthenian faithful in those localities where no church nor priest of their rite is available will conform to the Latin rite. The came concession applies to those who are unable to go to their churches without great inconvenience because of distance, although no one should be induced to change rites by this provision.

Article 27.   Marriage between Ruthenian and Latin Catholics is not prohibited, but a husband of the Latin rite may not follow the rite of his Ruthenian wife, nor a wife of the Latin rite follow the rite of her Ruthenian husband.

Article 34.   Children born in the United States of America of a father of the Latin rite and a mother of the Ruthenian rite are to be baptized according to the Latin rite because offspring should follow the rite of their father in all respects if he is of the Latin rite.

Article 35.   If the father should be of the Ruthenian rite and the mother of the Latin rite, the father is free to choose whether the child should be baptized by the Ruthenian rite or by the Latin rite, in case he so decides in consideration of his Latin-rite wife.

In the love of Christ, by which we the faithful of all rites are permanently bound, we consider these decisions necessary for the spiritual good and the health of the souls of the Ruthenian faithful residing in the United States of America. We have no doubt that they will receive these decisions taken on their behalf with gratitude and with perfect obedience.

The present letter and its every statute and content is not to be censured, impugned, called into question, or subjected to scrutiny for any reason whatsoever. . . .

Dated at Rome, in Saint Peter's, in the year of our Lord 1907, on the fourteenth day of June, the festal day of Saint Basil the Great, in the fourth year of our [Pius X] papacy.

the free," these lay leaders argued, "it would be ridiculous to support and work for a cause without representation."[4]

These varying levels of antagonism became especially apparent in 1907, when the Vatican finally appointed a bishop for America's Greek Catholics. Actually, even before the appointment was made, Carpatho-Rusyn clergy and lay leaders wanted the nominee to be from Hungary, while the Ukrainophile priests and their supporters quite naturally wanted their own. In the end, the advice of the influential Greek Catholic Metropolitan from Galicia, Andrej Šeptyc'kyj, seemed to have been decisive, because in 1907 the Vatican appointed a priest from Galicia, Soter Ortynsky, to be the first Greek Catholic bishop in America. Instead of improving the situation, however, Ortynsky's appointment only added more fuel to a fire that had already alienated most Carpatho-Rusyns from their Galician Ukrainian co-religionists.

Because he was from Galicia and seemed to associate himself with Ukrainians, Bishop Ortynsky was opposed by many Carpatho-Rusyns from Hungary, who almost immediately began an "anti-Ortynsky" campaign. Their opposition took on particular intensity when Ortynsky, although against his personal convictions, was called upon to enforce the provisions of the latest Vatican decree. This was contained in a papal letter known as the *Ea Semper*, which was made public less than one month after the bishop's arrival in the United States on September 16, 1907. The document was intended to regulate relations between Latin- and Greek (Byzantine)-rite Catholics, with the intention to preserve the "venerable liturgies of the Eastern churches." It also became clear, however, that a separate American Greek Catholic diocese was not to be established and that the first bishop, Ortynsky, was in effect to be only an auxiliary to the Latin-rite bishops where Rusyns lived. Furthermore, Greek Catholic priests were not to administer the sacrament of confirmation at baptism, married seminarians were not to be

16. Bishop Soter Ortynsky.

ordained, and new priests were not to be sent to the United States without the advance approval of the American Catholic hierarchy. To the accusations that Ortynsky was a Ukrainian, another epithet was added: that he was a Latinizer ready to give in to every wish of Rome.

In actual fact, Ortynsky protested to the Vatican, urging the repeal of the decree. Although his demand was ignored, those provisions of the *Ea Semper* decree which concerned traditional Greek Catholic practices, while left on the books, were not effectively enforced. Nonetheless, several Carpatho-Rusyn priests and lay leaders, most especially from the influential Greek Catholic Union fraternal society, remained profoundly angered with the decree and continued to heap abuse on Ortynsky in their publications. They were in particular critical when Ortynsky attempted to enforce one provision of the *Ea Semper* decree—abandonment of the trustee system of church ownership, whereby all title to church property would be deeded to the bishop. Most Carpatho-Rusyn parishes simply refused to do this,

[4] Michael Yuhasz in the *Amerikansky russky viestnik*, July 4, 1902, cited in John Slivaka, *Historical Mirror: Sources of the Rusin and Hungarian Greek Rite Catholics in the United States of America 1884-1963* (Brooklyn, N.Y., 1978), p. 32.

Major Carpatho-Rusyn Religious Affiliations in the United States

Church	Diocesan / Eparchial seat(s)	Founding date	First hierarch	Present hierarch(s)	Publications	Carpatho-Rusyn membership (estimate)
Byzantine Ruthenian Catholic Metropolitan Archdiocese (formerly Greek Catholic Exarchate of Pittsburgh)	Pittsburgh, Pennsylvania Passaic, New Jersey Parma, Ohio Van Nuys, California	1916/1924	Basil Takach	John Bilock Michael Dudick Andrew Pataki George Kuzma	*Byzantine Catholic World* *Eastern Catholic Life* *Horizons*	195,000
American Carpatho-Russian Orthodox Greek Catholic Church (formerly Carpatho-Russian Greek Catholic Diocese of the Eastern Rite)	Johnstown, Pennsylvania	1937	Orestes Chornock	Nicholas Smisko	*Church Messenger*	18,000
Orthodox Church in America (formerly Russian Orthodox Greek Catholic Church of America—the Metropolia)	Washington, D.C. Detroit, Michigan Pittsburgh, Pennsylvania New York, New York Dallas, Texas Philadelphia, Pennsylvania Sitka, Alaska San Francisco, California Hartford, Connecticut Ottawa, Ontario	1794 1916—Carpatho-Russian Exarchy (Stephan Dzubay) 1951—Carpatho-Russian People's Church (Andrew Šlepecky)	Ioasaf Bolotov	Theodosius Lazor Kyrill Yonchev Peter L'Huillier Dmitri Royster Herman Swaiko Gregory Afonsky Job Osacky Nathaniel Popp Tikhon Fitzgerald Seraphim Storheim	*Orthodox Church*	250,000
Russian Orthodox Church in the USA and Canada—the Patriarchal Parishes	New York, New York	1933 1943—Carpatho-Russian administration (Adam Philipovsky)	Benjamin Fedchenkov	Paul Ponomarev	*One Church*	8,000

and some even went to court over this issue.

The attacks on the unfortunate bishop did not subside, even after the Vatican passed two more favorable decrees. In May 1913, Ortynsky was finally given full episcopal power, and in August 1914, according to a new Vatican decree, the *Cum Episcopo*, jurisdictional relations between Roman and Byzantine-rite Greek Catholics were clarified. The intention was to safeguard Greek Catholics from the predominantly American Roman Catholic environment in which they operated. Then, in an attempt to quell further discontent arising from regional rivalries, Bishop Ortynsky appointed two Carpatho-Rusyns from Hungary, Father Alexander Dzubay as his vicar-general and Father Augustine Komporday as his chancellor.

None of these acts, however, seemed to allay the fears of the Carpatho-Rusyns. Led by lay leaders from the Greek Catholic Union, they continued to argue that they form a distinct nationality. "The Uhro-Rusins have wholly different customs from the Galicians; their church hymns are different; and even in the performance of ceremonies there are noticeable differences."[5] Furthermore, Galician Ukrainians were accused of putting "nationalistic aims" above religious concerns. Arguments such as these were used not only in 1913, they have been used ever since by Carpatho-Rusyn secular and clerical spokesmen as justification for maintaining their distinctiveness and distance from Ukrainian Americans. Therefore, the Carpatho-Rusyns could "under no consideration renounce their intention of having their own Uhro-Rusin bishop" nor "acquiesce to being ecclesiastically united with the Galician Ukrainians," in order that "under the guise of the Catholic Church they might be thrown into the slavery of Ukrainianism."[6]

In the midst of an increasingly tense atmosphere within the Greek Catholic Church, Bishop Ortynsky unexpectedly died in 1916. Realizing the regional qua national divisions between the Carpatho-Rusyns and Galician Ukrainians who, if "they were to be forcibly united, there would be no peace and order but perpetual wrangling

17. Father Gabriel Martyak.

through which the Catholic Church would lose considerably,"[7] the Vatican decided to create two ecclesiastical administrations for Eastern-rite Catholics in the United States. Thus, instead of a single episcopal successor to Ortynsky, two administrators were appointed: Father Gabriel Martyak for the Greek Catholics from Hungary and Father Peter Poniatyshyn for Greek Catholics from Galicia. Indeed, no parish was composed exclusively of families from one region or the other, so that there were some Rusyns from Hungary in Galician parishes and vice-versa. Moreover, those Lemkos who remained Greek Catholics came under the Galician jurisdiction.

Eventually, this division along regional lines came to be associated as well with self-imposed ethnonational distinctions. Thus, while the "Hungarian" Greek Catholic administrative jurisdiction included Slovaks as well as a few Magyars and Croats, it soon came to be ethnically associated with its Carpatho-Rusyn majority and was to be known as the Byzantine Ruthenian Catholic Church. Similarly, while the Galician Greek

[5] Petition of the Greek Catholic Union to the Apostolic Delegate to the United States (1913), cited in Slivka, *Historical Mirror*, p. 105.

[6] Slivka, *Historical Mirror*, p. 106.

[7] Slivka, *Historical Mirror*, p. 105.

18. Bishop Stephen (Alexander) Dzubay upon consecration in 1916.

Catholic administrative jurisdiction included Lemkos and some others who continued to identify themselves as Rusyns, sometimes even as Russians, the vast majority increasingly identified themselves ethnically as Ukrainians, so that the institution came to be known as the Ukrainian Catholic Church. Thus, the administrative division of 1916 was, in a sense, a latent recognition of the deep ethnic, cultural, and psychological differences that had existed from the very beginning among America's Eastern-rite Catholics. This move toward separation ushered in a new period of peace and stability within the two branches—Byzantine Ruthenian and Ukrainian—of the Greek or Byzantine-rite Catholic Church.

Not that this was the end of problems which could still deeply effect the church's development. In fact, already by 1916, a new crisis arose within

the Byzantine Ruthenian administration. The vicar-general, Alexander Dzubay, became a leading candidate for bishop after Ortynsky's death. Moreover, Dzubay had the support of the powerful Greek Catholic Union. And as the senior member of the clergy, he expected at the very least to be appointed administrator for Carpatho-Rusyns from Hungary. When he was passed over in favor of Martyak, the discontented Dzubay decided to leave the Catholic church altogether and to become an Orthodox monk. In rapid succession, he entered a monastery and took the name Stephen (July 30, 1916); he was elevated the very next day to archimandrite (July 31); he then agreed to be appointed bishop of a "Carpatho-Russian Subdiocese in Pittsburgh," and in the presence of the head of the Russian Orthodox Church in America and other Orthodox bishops was consecrated at St. Nicholas Orthodox Cathedral in New York City (August 20).

As Bishop Stephen, Dzubay established his residence in Pittsburgh and immediately began a campaign to convert Byzantine Ruthenian Catholics to Orthodoxy. He was able to convince several churches in the Pittsburgh area to go over to Orthodoxy, but he was less successful in obtaining a jurisdictionally-independent Carpatho-Russian diocese within the Russian Orthodox Church. Foreseeing this unlikelihood, Dzubay decided in late 1922 to consecrate Father Adam Philipovsky as head of a Carpatho-Russian Exarchy, comprising between 30 to 40 parishes of mostly recent converts to Orthodoxy from among Lemko immigrants from Galicia. Following an independent course, this exarchy never grew in size, and Bishop Philipovsky was from the outset plagued by his participation in the jurisdictional disputes that characterized Russian Orthodoxy in America during the years after World War I. The outcome of those disputes was the eventual creation of three separate jurisdictions: (1) the Russian Orthodox Greek Catholic Church, which remained loyal to the mother church in Russia, although it insisted on the status of autonomy, thereby becoming popularly known as the Metropolia; (2) the Russian Orthodox Church Outside Russia, which refused to recognize the patriarch in Soviet Russia and prefered to be ruled in the traditional collegial or synodal manner, thereby becoming popularly known as the Synod; and (3) the

Russian Orthodox Church in the U.S.A., comprised of parishes which remained directly under the authority of the patriarch in Moscow, thereby becoming popularly known as the Patriarchal Exarchate. As we shall see, it was not uncommon for parishes, priests, and hierarchs to move from one Orthodox jurisdiction to another, moves that were often accompanied by great controversy and that in some cases led to legal battles in the American court system.

As for Bishop Dzubay, he soon became frustrated with the failure to create a serious Carpatho-Rusyn Orthodox diocese which he expected to head. Consequently, he turned his attention to the Russian Orthodox Church as a whole. Taking advantage of the breakdown in communications with the Russian homeland (ruled after 1917 by a Soviet regime) and the resultant confusion within the Orthodox movement in the United States, Dzubay convoked an Orthodox Council (sobor) in October 1922 and proclaimed himself to be "acting head" of the entire Russian Orthodox Church in America. Although followed by several priests, in early 1924 Dzubay nonetheless relinquished his claims and recognized the newly elected Orthodox Metropolitan Platon. Frustrated at every turn in his overambitious bid for power, by late 1924 Dzubay renounced his Orthodox bishopric, begged for forgiveness, and returned to the fold of Byzantine-rite Catholicism. He spent the last eight years of his life as a secluded penitent in a Roman Catholic monastery.

Dzubay's career is of interest because it reveals a pattern that began to take shape already in 1891 with Father Toth, and which has continued in some cases down to the present day. In effect, Orthodoxy became the safety-valve for discontented Greek/Byzantine Ruthenian Catholics, both among the clergy and lay parishioners. Whenever there was reason for discontent and for whatever the cause: whether threats to Eastern religious tradition; refusal to relinquish parish-owned church property; frustrated personal ambition; or simply dislike for the local priest, Byzantine Ruthenian Catholics could always count on being accepted (and in the case of some priests often being given high posts) within one of the Orthodox churches.

Having reviewed these early years of the Carpatho-Rusyn religious community, one might conclude that because the Greek (Byzantine-rite)

Catholic Church was being constantly rent by internal regional and national divisions and by external pressure from an antagonistic American Catholic clergy, the number of its adherents was continually on the decline. At the same time, its Orthodox rivals—not to mention the Latin-rite churches and Protestant sects—were gaining at the expense of the Greek Catholics. In order not to get the wrong impression, however, one should remember that all these developments were taking place precisely at a time when Carpatho-Rusyns were flocking to America in larger numbers than ever before or after. The result was that, despite defections, the Greek Catholic Church did actually continue to grow, so that by the time Ortynsky received full episcopal powers in 1913, he had jurisdiction over 152 churches, 154 priests, and 500,000 communicants from Galicia, Bukovina, and Hungary.

The next important development came in 1924, when the Vatican decided to replace the temporary Byzantine-rite administrators with bishops. Father Basil Takach from the Eparchy of Mukačevo, at the time within the borders of the

19. Bishop Basil Takach (photo by Parry).

Cum Data Fuerit Decree

(Excerpts from the first published version in the *Leader/Vožd'*, II, 12, December 1930, pp. 20-23)

Article 1. The nomination of the bishops is reserved to the Apostolic See.

Article 6. In order to safeguard the temporal goods of the Church, the bishops shall not permit rectors of churches or boards of administrators to possess in their own right goods contributed in any manner by the faithful. They shall insist that the property be held in a manner that makes it safe for the church according to the laws of the various States. They shall issue rules concerning the administration of the church property.

Article 12. Before the Greek-Ruthenian Church has a sufficient number of priests educated in the United States, the bishops may through the Sacred Congregation for the Oriental Church ask the Greek-Ruthenian bishops of Europe to send them priests. Priests who are not called by the bishops or sent by the Sacred Congregation, but come to the United States of their own accord, cannot be given faculties by the Greek-Ruthenian bishops in the United States, either for saying Mass, or for the administration of the Sacraments, or for any ecclesiastical work. **The priests who wish to come to the United States and stay there must be celibates.**

Article 37. **Associations of the faithful of the Greek-Ruthenian rite shall be under the vigilance of the bishops,** who shall name the priest who is to have charge of these associations, in order to avoid any abuses with regard to faith, morals, or discipline. Hence it is praiseworthy on the part of the faithful to join associations which have been formed, or at least approved, by ecclesiastical authority. **The faithful should be on their guard, however, against associations which are secret, condemned, seditious, suspect, or which seek to elude the supervision of lawful ecclesiastical authority.**

Likewise Catholic newspapers, magazines, and periodicals are under the supervision of the bishop, and without his permission priests should neither write in them nor manage them.

His Holiness, Pius XI, ratified and confirmed all the above provisions in the audience of 9 February 1929, and ordered the present Decree to be issued, to be effective for ten years.

---

new republic of Czechoslovakia, was named bishop of the newly created Pittsburgh Exarchate, which was to have jurisdiction over all Byzantine-rite Catholics from the former Kingdom of Hungary. Upon its establishment, the exarchate comprised 155 churches, 129 priests, and 288,390 parishioners. Simultaneously, Father Constantine Bohachevsky was named bishop for Byzantine-rite Catholics from Galicia and Bukovina. His diocese, soon to be called the Ukrainian Catholic Church, had its seat in Philadelphia and jurisdiction over 144 churches, 129 priests, and 237,495 parishioners. With this move, Byzantine-rite Catholics gained the legal and structural institutions they had so long desired, although they were split into two jurisdictions depending on whether they originated from north or south of the crest of the Carpathians. This meant that the Lemkos who came from Galicia (that is, those who did not already convert to Orthodoxy) were now split from their fellow Carpatho-Rusyns from former Hungary and instead were jurisdictionally united with other Byzantine-rite Catholics from Galicia, who more and more identified with a Ukrainian ethnic identity. On the other hand, the regional qua national dissension that had marked Greek (Byzantine-rite) Catholic church life until World War I seemed to be overcome, since the bulk of the Carpatho-Rusyns were now separated from the Galician Ukrainians.

This promising beginning toward stability was shattered as early as 1929, however, when in February of that year the Vatican issued (but did not make public) a new decree, the *Cum Data Fuerit.* This decree basically reiterated many of the provisions of the 1907 *Ea Semper,* which in any case had never been strictly enforced. For instance, Bishop Takach had even consecrated married priests during the early years of his episcopacy. The *Cum Data Fuerit* was, therefore, an attempt to assure that the Vatican's legal norms be followed, and this time the bishop decided to try to enforce the decree's provisions. Of the several jurisdictional and administrative matters that were dealt with in the *Cum Data Fuerit,* it was the reaffirmation of celibacy, the attack on the trusteeship system of holding church property, and the ban against interference in church affairs by fraternal organizations which led to almost immediate conflict with several priests and lay leaders, especially in the powerful Greek Catholic Union.

For the next eight years, 1930 to 1938, the Byzantine Ruthenian Catholic Church (as the Pittsburgh Exarchate later came to be known) was rent by an almost unending series of conflicts that set priests, fraternal societies, parishioners, even family members against each other in what came to be known as the celibacy controversy. In fact, celibacy was only one of the issues, the other causes of the controversy being the problem of ecclesiastical discipline, rivalry between clergy originating from differing eparchies in Europe (Mukačevo versus Prešov), interference of secular societies in church affairs, and the trustee system of holding church property.

The trouble began when three Rusyn-American seminarians, having completed their studies in the European homeland and having married, returned to the United States. They requested ordination, but Bishop Takach refused. An inquiry made by Father Orestes Chornock of Bridgeport, Connecticut (the parish priest of one of the semi-

narians) as to why ordination was denied led to friction with the bishop, to the publication in late 1930 of the *Cum Data Fuerit* decree, and to the call by some priests, joined by the laity and the Greek Catholic Union, to struggle against the "unjust" denial of Greek Catholic (Byzantine Ruthenian) religious tradition. Because of his insubordination, Father Chornock together with four other priests, including the Greek Catholic Union's editor, Father Stefan Varzaly, were suspended from the priesthood and then excommunicated. These acts only added more fuel to an expanding fire that grew in intensity after the Greek Catholic Union and its so-called Committee for the Defense of the Eastern Rite (KOVO, established 1932) joined the fray, and after individual parishes refused to turn over their property to the bishop.

The next few years were marked by often harsh and libellous charges and countercharges in the fraternal and religious press between the "rebellious" or "tradition-minded" priests around Chornock and Varzaly on the one hand, and the

20. Church Congress in Pittsburgh, November 22-24, 1937, which proclaimed the existence of an independent diocese that became the Carpatho-Russian Orthodox Greek Catholic Church. Seated in the front row; the Reverend Orestes Chornock (behind the flowers), flanked by the Reverend Ireneus Dolhy (on the left) and the Reverend Stephen Varzaly (on the right).

21. Bishop Orestes Chornock upon consecration in 1938.

22. St. John the Baptist Church, Arctic Street, Bridgeport, Connecticut. First episcopal residence of the American Carpatho-Russian Orthodox Greek Catholic Church.

Byzantine Ruthenian hierarchy and priests loyal to Bishop Takach on the other. With no solution in sight, the dissident priests, led by Chornock, Varzaly, and Peter Molchany, met in early 1936 to set the groundwork for a church body that would be independent of Rome. In November 1937, they were joined by several laymen, and meeting in Pittsburgh they formed a church council which declared its abrogation of union with Rome and its return to the "ancestral faith" of the Carpatho-Rusyn people. The new organization, which attracted about 30,000 former Byzantine Catholics, was called the Carpatho-Russian Greek Catholic Diocese of the Eastern Rite.

This body claimed to be the "true," or Orthodox, Greek Catholic Church, which was simply maintaining or restoring traditional Eastern-rite practices. The next question concerned juris-dictional affiliation. Having just rejected Rome, the new church was not about to ally itself with the Russian Orthodox Church either. Its leaders were well aware of the difficulties encountered by Bishop Dzubay and his successor in trying to

maintain Rusyn religious traditions and a distinct Carpatho-Russian diocese within the Orthodox Metropolia. In fact, the protest movement of the 1930s was heralded by the slogan: "ani do Rimu, ani do Moskvi" (neither Rome nor Moscow). Instead, the new church received its canonical jurisdiction directly from the Ecumenical Patriarch in Constantinople, a development that was made possible through the good offices of the Greek Orthodox Archbishop of New York, Athenagoras, who later liked to refer to himself as the "godfather of the Carpatho-Russian diocese." Thus, in 1938, Father Chornock travelled to Con-stantinople, where he was consecrated bishop. Although technically subordinate to the Greek Orthodox Archbishop of America, the Carpatho-Russian Greek Catholic Diocese of the Eastern Rite became, in fact, an independent and self-governing body. Bishop Chornock chose his own parish in Bridgeport, Connecticut as the first diocesan seat, but in 1950 (after a particularly bitter court battle in which the parish was lost) the diocesan headquarters were transferred to Johns-

28. Christ the Saviour Cathedral, Johnstown, Pennsylvania, the cathedral church of the American Carpatho-Russian Orthodox Greek Catholic Diocese, built 1954.

that time, as discussions about eastern and western ecclesiastical unity become more serious, the issues over which the former antagonistic contenders fought so intensely seem no longer to have any validity.

Any description of religious life among Carpatho-Rusyns would not be complete without a few words about converts to Roman Catholicism and Protestantism. As we have seen, during the early years of the Greek/Byzantine Ruthenian Catholic Church, many Carpatho-Rusyns—some estimates state as many as one-third of the total number—passed over to the Latin rite. This often occurred because there were no local Byzantine Ruthenian Catholic churches or because in mixed marriages the "more American" Latin rite seemed preferable. It was not until 1929 that this problem was clarified. Actually, the otherwise controversial *Cum Data Fuerit* decree, which fuelled anew the celibacy controversy, was primarily concerned with

regulating relations between the Latin and Byzantine rites. Henceforth, it was prescribed that children of mixed Latin- and Byzantine-rite parents follow the rite of the father, and this act largely stemmed the flow of changes to the Latin rite.

Ironically, attitudes toward the two rites of the Catholic Church have altered dramatically in the past three decades. The reason has to do with Vatican Council II, which between 1962 and 1965 instituted several changes in the Roman Catholic Church, including the replacement of Latin with local languages (generally English in the United States) and the introduction of congregational singing, which until then seemed to be the preserve of Protestants. The ecumenical thrust of Vatican II also helped to end the former condescending attitudes on the part of Latin-rite clergy toward their Byzantine-rite brethren. Since at least the 1970s, some Latin-rite Catholics of various ethnic backgrounds, reacting to what they perceive as a loss of tradition, have begun to attend Byzantine Ruthenian churches which are perceived to be more tradition-minded. Thus, the traditions that the Byzantine Ruthenian Catholics were once so anxious to give up are now seen by many Roman Catholics as an attractive antidote to the otherwise ritualized blandness of American Catholicism.

In the early years of this century, Protestant missionary activity was widespread among newly arrived immigrants, although it was not particularly successful among Slavs. Moreover, as we have seen, Carpatho-Rusyn Greek Catholics always had the safety-valve of Orthodoxy to turn to whenever their discontent was not allayed. Nonetheless, some Carpatho-Rusyns (the actual number or even an estimate is difficult if not impossible to determine) did join mainstream American Protestant churches, especially Baptist ones, where they became quickly assimilated, losing all ties with the ethnic identity of their forebears. One exception was the group in Proctor, Vermont, which founded a fundamentalist Bible-reading sect with branches in Naugatuck, Connecticut and Passaic, New

30. Archbishop Theodosius Lazor, Metropolitan of the Orthodox Church in America.

Jersey. Through its publication, *Proroczeskoe svitlo/The Prophetic Light* (Proctor, Vt., 1921-53), the group was able to maintain for many decades a sense of affinity with its Carpatho-Rusyn origins. Descendants of the original group continue to meet in southern Connecticut and the New York City-New Jersey metropolitan area.

The strong religious orientation of the Rusyn-American community has produced individuals who have played a significant role in church affairs beyond as well as within the group's own denominations. Miriam Teresa Demjanovich was the daughter of Rusyn immigrants from the Prešov Region of eastern Slovakia. Before her untimely death at the age of 27, she had become a Roman Catholic Sister of Charity and author of a series of "spiritual conferences" published a year after her death in English and several other languages under the title, *Greater Perfection* (1928). Inspired by her life and writings, a Sister Miriam Teresa League was established in 1945 to work on behalf of her beatification which, should it occur, would make her the first female American saint of Slavic descent in the Catholic Church.

Priests of Carpatho-Rusyn descent still play a leading role in traditional Orthodox churches. Archbishop Theodosius Lazor, the son of Carpatho-Rusyn immigrants from the Lemko Region,

29. Sister Miriam Teresa Demjanovich.

31. Bishop Laurus Škurla, Diocese of Syracuse and Jordanville, Russian Orthodox Church Abroad—the Synod. He was born in the Carpatho-Rusyn village of Ladomirová in the Prešov Region.

holds the highest office in the large Orthodox Church in America. Another is Bishop Laurus Škurla, who heads the Diocese of Syracuse in the Russian Orthodox Church Abroad—the Synod. Although very few Rusyn Americans are members of this Orthodox jurisdiction, Bishop Laurus became associated with its Holy Trinity Monastery during the 1920s when it was still located in his native village of Ladomirová in the Prešov Region of Slovakia. The community of monks transferred to Jordanville in upper New York state after World War II. Bishop Laurus resides at the Jordanville monastery, which has become a mecca for Russian Orthodox traditionalists, including fervent supporters like the writer Alexander Solzhenitsyn and the conductor-cellist Mystyslav Rostropovich.

Perhaps the most influential American of Carpatho-Rusyn background active in religion is the evangelist minister Joseph W. Tkach. The son of Rusyn immigrants from the Prešov region of eastern Slovakia, Tkach became in 1986 pastor general of the California-based Worldwide Church of God. With 94,000 members in 120 countries, Tkach reaches his faithful—as well as millions of others—through his role as editor-in-chief of the widely-distributed magazine, *The Plain Truth*, and the syndicated nationwide news-oriented television program, "The World Tomorrow." It is interesting to note that in 1992, when the Worldwide Church of God began to proselytize in the former Soviet Union, it launched its work in Ukraine's Transcarpathia where, as the church's official newspaper reported, "the somber crowd listened with great interest" as the preacher from America "spoke about Mr. Tkach's Rusyn roots."[9]

[9] *The World Wide News* (Pasadena, Calif.), October 6, 1992, p. 2.

32. Joseph W. Tkach, Pastor General of the Worldwide Church of God.

Chapter 5

Organizational Life

Thrust into a world that was politically, economically, culturally, and linguistically alien, the early Carpatho-Rusyn immigrants, like other newcomers to America's shores, sought ways to cushion the psychological impact of their exposure to a new environment. This is not to say that all Carpatho-Rusyns felt lost and alienated in America. Some, whose intent was often to make money as quickly as possible, adapted easily and achieved their goals. Most, however, tried in some way to interact socially with their fellow immigrants and to recreate, in however rudimentary a fashion, the Old-World environment they had left behind.

At first, the boardinghouses, grocery stores, local taverns, and, of course, the church—at least on Sundays and holidays—provided the setting for social interaction. Next to the church, the most important organizations were the fraternal societies and brotherhoods. Actually, these arose not so much because of their potential social function, but rather for very practical needs. In a foreign land, where most immigrant workers had insufficient funds to protect themselves in case of industrial accidents or other mishaps, the fraternal organizations were able to provide a minimal but nonetheless important source of financial help in times of distress. And although life insurance policies and workmen's compensation programs provided some financial security, the newspaper, youth clubs, sports organizations, and social gatherings also

sponsored by the fraternals contributed a measure of psychological security for immigrants in the company of their fellow-countrymen. Thus, it was not long before the fraternal societies saw themselves as defenders of Carpatho-Rusyn culture and religion, so that next to the churches they were to become the most influential force directing the destiny of the community in the United States.

Initially, all Greek (Byzantine-rite) Catholic immigrants, whether they were from the old Hungarian Kingdom or Austrian Galicia, belonged to the same fraternals. But before long friction developed among the varying factions. There were several kinds of differences. These included: (1) regional differences—Galicians vs. the *uhorci* (those from old Hungary); (2) religious differences—Greek/Byzantine Catholics vs. Orthodox; and (3) national differences—Rusynophiles vs. Russophiles, Ukrainophiles, Slovakophiles, or Magyarones. Splits resulted and new fraternals were created to represent each of the many orientations that evolved in the community. This fragmentation actually occurred rather quickly, so that by the 1890s, each of the various regional, religious, and national groups had its own distinct fraternal organization. Moreover, this rather rapid growth of fraternal societies seemed to be a particularly American phenomenon, especially for Carpatho-Rusyns who, with very few exceptions, did not have similar organizations in the European homeland before 1918.

The first fraternal organization was the St. Nicholas Brotherhood, founded in 1885 in the coal mining town of Shenandoah, Pennsylvania by the pioneer Greek Catholic priest in America, Father John Volansky. Although the brotherhood was shortlived, lasting only until 1889 when Father Volansky returned to Europe, it nonetheless was part of an active community which also published the first newspaper, *Ameryka* (Shenandoah, Pa., 1886-90), as an "organ for Rusyn immigrants from Galicia and Hungary."

Following the demise of the St. Nicholas Brotherhood, parish-based lodges did continue to survive, but many Carpatho-Rusyns began to join recently founded Slovak fraternals, such as the First Catholic Slovak Union Jednota (est. 1890) and the Pennsylvania Slovak Roman and Greek Catholic Union (est. 1891). It was in part the movement of Rusyns into Slovak Roman Catholic fraternals that highlighted the need for a specific Carpatho-Rusyn organization. During a meeting of 14 Greek Catholic priests who in December 1891 had gathered to protest their treatment by the

Vatican and by the American Roman Catholic Church, it was decided to establish a single fraternal society and to publish a newspaper. This goal came to fruition a few months later, when a group of 6 Greek Catholic priests, joined by representatives of 14 local brotherhoods, met in Wilkes Barre, Pennsylvania, to form one body that would unite them all. They named it the Greek Catholic Union of Russian [Rusyn] Brotherhoods (Sojedninenije Greko-Kaftoličeskich Russkich Bratstv), and according to its founding charter of February 14, 1892, set as its goals: to strive for unity among the majority of "Greek Catholics who speak Rusyn"; to provide insurance for its members; to encourage education and promote the construction of schools and churches; and to provide a plan to protect widows, orphans, and the indigent. The first chairman was John Zinčak-Smith, and the first editor of its newspaper, the *Amerikansky russky viestnik* (Wilkes Barre, Scranton, New York, Pittsburgh, and Homestead, Pa., 1892-1952), was Pavel Zatkovich, both Carpatho-Rusyns from Hungary. The Greek Catholic Union (hereafter GCU) began in 1892 with 743 members in 14 lodges. During

33. John Zinčak-Smith.

34. Pavel Zatkovich.

35. Insurance policy of the Greek Catholic Union, dated 1927. This attractively designed policy, measuring 14 x 24 inches, included texts in English and Rusyn, both in the Latin and Cyrillic alphabets.

the next two decades, which coincided with the height of immigration from Europe, the GCU grew accordingly, and by 1928, at its height, it counted 120,000 members in 1,328 lodges. In 1905, it opened new headquarters with offices and printing facilities in Homestead, Pennsylvania. To this day, the GCU has remained the largest Carpatho-Rusyn fraternal organization, and during the last two decades under George Batyko it has maintained a steady membership while increasing substantially its financial base. By the time of its centenary celebrations in 1992, the GCU had 40,000 members (holding 50,000 certificates) in 120 lodges and assets of $210,000,000.

Because of its rapid growth, the GCU had to accommodate Byzantine-rite Catholics of various backgrounds, and its newspaper, the *Amerikansky russky viestnik,* was even published for several decades in two editions, a Carpatho-Rusyn edition in the Cyrillic alphabet, and a so-called "Slavish" edition in the Latin alphabet with a language that was a transitional Eastern Slovak/ Carpatho-Rusyn dialect. From the very beginning, however, the leadership and activity of the GCU was basically concerned with Greek (Byzantine-rite) Catholics of Rusyn background from south of the Carpathian Mountains. Consequently, many neighboring Slovaks of the Byzantine-rite avoided the GCU and instead joined the First Catholic Slovak Union Jednota and the Pennsylvania Slovak Roman and Greek Catholic Union.

The next group to defect was the Galicians, who became disenchanted with what they called the Magyarone-dominated leadership of the GCU. Upon the initiative of four priests from Galicia—Gregory Hrushka, Ivan Konstankevych, Theodore Obushkevych, and Ambrose Poliansky—a new "Russian," later Rusyn National Association (Russkij/Rus'kyj Narodnyj Sojuz) was founded in Shamokin, Pennsylvania in 1894. Hrushka became the founding editor of its newspaper, *Svoboda* (Jersey City, N.J., 1894-present), and by the turn of the century this organization was reinforced by nationally conscious Galician-Ukrainian immigrants who, in 1914, changed its name to the Ukrainian National Association. This body is today the largest secular Ukrainian organization in the United States.

As a result of the increasing Ukrainophile orientation of the Rusyn National Association, dis-

contented Galician Russophiles like Father Theodore Obushkevych were joined by sympathizers in the GCU who met in Hazelton, Pennsylvania, in September 1901, to form the Russian Brotherhood Organization (Obščestvo Russkich Bratstv). Zinčak-Smith, the first chairman of the GCU, was chosen to head this new group, while a former member of the Rusyn National Association, Viktor P. Hladik, became founding editor of the society's newspaper, *Pravda/The Truth* (New York, Olyphant, Philadelphia, Pottstown, Pa., Mogodore, Oh., 1902-present). At the height of its growth, during the late 1930s, the organization had around 13,000 members in 264 lodges. By 1992, however, the membership had decreased to less than 2,000, and it does not seem there is any potential for future growth.

Finally, those parishes which Father Alexis Toth brought over to Orthodoxy felt the need for their own organization. Led by Toth and laymen like Ivan Repa and Ivan Pivovarnik, a small group met in Wilkes Barre in April 1895 to form the Russian Orthodox Catholic Mutual Aid Society (Russkoe Pravoslavnoe Obščestvo Vzaimopomošči). Led for many years by the determined Russophile, Father Peter Kohanik, this group through its newspaper, *Svit/The Light* (Wilkes Barre, 1894-present), and annual calendars tried to offset the Greek Catholic societies and to preserve the "Orthodox faith and Russian nationality" of its Carpatho-Rusyn membership. The society never regained the nearly 10,000 members it had in 1918, and by 1992, it had only 2,300 members in 100 lodges.

Thus, already at the beginning of the twentieth century, several insurance and fraternal organizations existed which represented the various national, regional, and religious affiliations of the Carpatho-Rusyn immigrant community. The Greek Catholic Union was to include primarily Carpatho-Rusyns and some Slovaks from the pre-1918 Hungarian Kingdom and was to follow either a separatist Rusyn or, especially during the 1930s, a Russophile national orientation. The other groups initially attracted immigrants from Galicia, including many Lemkos, and were to identify either with the Russian nationality (Society of Russian Brotherhoods, Russian Orthodox Mutual Aid Society) or Ukrainian (Rusyn/Ukrainian National Association) nationalities.

36. Headquarters of the Greek Catholic Union, Beaver, Pennsylvania, opened 1987.

Through its financial power and newspaper circulation (at one time as high as 120,000), the Greek Catholic Union was to wield great influence over Carpatho-Rusyn religious and political activity. In general, the GCU defended what it considered to be the religious and cultural interests of the Carpatho-Rusyn community and it adopted a traditionalist position, avidly opposing the "Latinizing" decrees passed down by the Vatican. Although during the 1890s the GCU worked to counteract the Orthodox "schism" led by the Reverend Toth, by the early twentieth century it had already begun unwittingly to aid that movement by its opposition to many of the policies of the Greek Catholic hierarchs, especially those of the first bishop, the Reverend Soter Ortynsky. In fact, from the very first day of his arrival in America in 1907, Ortynsky and *Amerikansky russky viestnik* editor Pavel Zatkovich became alienated from each other, thereby initiating a pattern of friction between the GCU and the church that it ostensibly defended. From the pages of its official newspaper, the GCU led an almost unending attack against the policies of

the new bishop, holding him accountable for enforcing the provisions of the Vatican's 1907 *Ea Semper* decree and accusing him of supporting, with the help of his fellow Galician priests and lay supporters, the Ukrainian "separatist movement."

It was precisely the GCU's antagonistic policy toward the Greek Catholic Church leadership that contributed to the growth of another Carpatho-Rusyn fraternal, the United Societies of Greek Catholic Religion (Sobranije Greko-Katholičeskich Cerkovnych Bratstv). This fraternal had actually come into being as early as 1903, when parishioners of the St. Nicholas parish in the Pittsburgh suburb of McKeesport, Pennsylvania broke away from the GCU. Although initially a local organization, after 1909 lodges were established outside of McKeesport (ironically, the first of these was as far away as Stockett, Montana), so that by 1915 there were 73 lodges with over 2,000 members. From the beginning, the United Societies included primarily Carpatho-Rusyns from the old Hungarian Kingdom, but unlike its older and larger rival, the GCU, it remained loyal to Bishop Ortynsky,

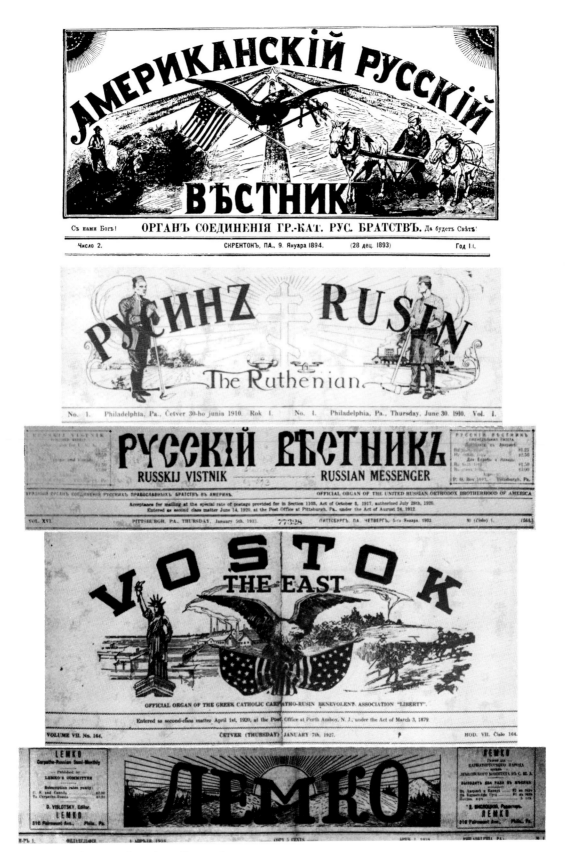

37. Early mastheads of Rusyn-American fraternal newspapers.

staunchly supporting him, his successors, and the official policies of the Greek Catholic Church. This approach was elaborated upon in the newspapers of the United Societies, including *Rusin/The Ruthenian* (Philadelphia and Pittsburgh, 1910-16), edited by Father Joseph Hanulya, and its successor *Prosvita/The Englightenment* (McKeesport, Pa., 1917-present), edited for its first 15 years by Father Valentine Gorzo. By 1992, the United Societies claimed 3,970 members in 40 lodges.

Meanwhile, throughout the whole pre-World War I period, the GCU remained in opposition to the Greek Catholic Church leadership under Bishop Ortynsky. It even contributed indirectly to Father Dzubay's defection to Orthodoxy. The GCU had touted Dzubay as the most able candidate to succeed Bishop Ortynsky after his death in 1916. When that did not happen, the discontented priest, who was convinced that he was supported by the community, turned to the Russian Orthodox Church where, as we have seen, he obtained an appointment as bishop. While the GCU did not follow Dzubay's example of defection from the Greek Catholic Church, it nonetheless remained ready to react whenever it perceived that the religious and cultural interests of the Carpatho-Rusyn community were threatened. For a while at least, interest (or interference) in church affairs in America was replaced by a growing concern with the fate of the homeland, and as we shall see in Chapter 8 below, the GCU was particularly influential during the international events of 1918-1919, which resulted in the incorporation of Carpatho-Rusyns living south of the Carpathians into Czechoslovakia.

By the 1930s, however, religious questions were once again the focus of attention, and it was during that decade that the GCU was to play its last truly dominant role in the life of Carpatho-Rusyns in America. The organization had been badly hit by the effects of the economic depression after 1929, when the failure of banks where it had invested funds threatened the fraternal's very existence. In this period of uncertainty and economic crisis, the GCU needed something to rally the support of its leaders and membership, and it seemed that that something was the celibacy issue. Whatever the motivation, the GCU soon found itself again embroiled in religious issues as it took up the defense of the married priesthood and other

38. Michael Yuhasz, Sr.

39. Dr. Peter I. Zeedick.

Lawrence A. Goga is particularly active, organizes several social functions, sponsors a Rusyn cultural exhibit at the annual Minneapolis folk festival, and publishes a newsletter, *Trembita* (Minneapolis, Minn., 1987-present).

Those Carpatho-Rusyn immigrants from Galicia known as Lemkos have felt the need to have their own organizations. A Lemko's Committee was established as early as 1922, whose primary function was to inform fellow Lemkos about developments in the homeland through the newspapers *Lemkovščyna* (New York, 1922-23) and *Lemko* (New York, Philadelphia, and Cleveland, 1928-39), edited respectively by the cultural activists Dr. Simeon Pysh and Dmitry Vislocky (pseud. Van'o Hunjanka). More intense organizational activity did not begin in the United States, however, but in Canada, where in early 1929, the first Lemko Council came into existence in Winnipeg, Manitoba. Several other branches of such councils were soon formed in other Canadian and especially American cities. By 1931, representatives of the branches met in Cleveland to unite them into a single Lemko Association (Lemko Sojuz) for the United States and Canada, and to adopt the newspaper *Lemko* as their official organ.

By the late 1930s, the focal point for Lemko

47. Carpatho-Russian American Center, Yonkers, New York, built 1939.

activity moved eastward from Cleveland to the New York City area. In 1939, the newspaper *Lemko* was merged with the recently founded *Karpatska Rus'* (Yonkers, N.Y., 1938-present), which was to be edited for its first two decades by the group's most prolific postwar spokesman, Dr. Simeon Pysh. To accommodate the community's increasing social and cultural needs, members of the local branch of the Lemko Association joined with members of the Russian Orthodox Catholic Mutual Aid Society to construct the Carpatho-Russian American Center. Opened in 1938, in the New York City suburb of Yonkers, the C-RA Center was from the outset popularly known as "Lemko Hall," even though it has never been owned by the Lemko Association. Since its establishment, the center, with its large banquet hall, performing stage, restaurant-tavern, and picnic grounds, has promoted social and cultural activity (including Lemko-Rusyn language classes and theatrical performances) and it has housed the Lemko Association and its newspaper, *Karpats'ka Rus'*. The Lemko Association no longer has a building in its original Cleveland home, although smaller Lemko clubs still exist in Ansonia and Bridgeport, Connecticut.

Especially popular is the Lemko Park in Monroe, New York, opened in 1958. With this park, older immigrants obtained what they call their own *vatra*, or fireside hearth, where they could spend their retirement years in the warm surrounding of friends. The park also became the site of the Talerhof Memorial, dedicated in 1964 to the "martyrdom" of thousands of Carpatho-Rusyns in Galicia at the hands of Austro-Hungarian

46. Dr. Simeon Pysh.

48. Lemko Hall, the headquarters of the Lemko National Home in Cleveland, Ohio, from 1949 to 1986.

authorities during the early years of World War I. As part of the remembrance, a pilgrimage with religious services (usually led by an Orthodox bishop of the Patriarchal Exarchate) is held annually at Pentecost *(Rusalja)*. Lemko Park also has a resort with hotel facilities and an amphitheater where every summer since 1969 a Carpatho-Russian festival takes place.

From the very outset, some Lemko Association spokespersons have been anti-clerical in orientation, even though most of its members were and still are Byzantine Catholic or Orthodox parishioners. The organization's publications have also been sympathetic to leftist political ideologies, making it the only segment of the Carpatho-Rusyn immigration to speak—at least until 1989—with sympathy about Communism, the Soviet Union, and its east-central European allies. Pro-Soviet attitudes were especially evident during the depression decade of the 1930s and World War II, although since then the group has often altered its views. During the 1960s, for instance, the editor of *Karpatska Rus'*, Stefan M. Kitchura, criticized Communist rule in the homeland and tried to have the

Lemko Association cooperate with anti-Soviet, Ukrainian-oriented Lemko-American groups. As a result, he was removed from the editorship and started instead his own organ, *Lemkovina* (Yonkers, N.Y., 1971-82). The Lemko Association, on the other hand, returned to a pro-Soviet stance. As for the problem of national identity, the group's publications have provided at various times differing and even contradictory explanations: that Lemkos form a distinct Slavic people; that as "Carpatho-Russians" they are part of one Russian nation; or that they are a branch of East Slavs most closely related to Ukrainians.

The seeming contradiction between church membership and the affirmation of pro-Soviet attitudes on the one hand, and confusion with respect to ethnic identity on the other, may possibly be explained by the ideology of Pan-Slavism. Like their nineteenth-century forebears in Europe, Lemko Association spokespersons felt that the unity of all Slavs was the ultimate ideal. In the twentieth century, only the might of the Soviet Union seemed to make such unity possible. Therefore, any threat to Soviet rule in east-central Europe was to be viewed as a potential threat to the greater goal of Slavic unity, which must be preserved at all costs. As a corollary to such views, the Soviet Union was viewed as the embodiment of Russia and of all Rus' peoples, including those from the Carpathians. It is in this sense, therefore, that the Lemko Association was ideologically pro-Soviet.

The Lemko Association's main goals have been to educate its members about their homeland through the publication of books, annual almanacs, and newspapers. Other Rusyn-American periodicals have gone to English, but the Lemko Association has used the native language (Lemko Region dialect) in the Cyrillic alphabet for the longest time. For instance, the official newspaper *Karpatska Rus'* added an English section for the first time only in the early 1980s. In an attempt to attract younger members, several exclusively English-language publications were started—the *Lemko Youth Journal* (Yonkers, N.Y., 1960-64), *Carpatho-Russian American* (Yonkers, N.Y., 1968-69), *Karpaty* (Yonkers, N.Y., 1978-79)—but these have been unable to survive for long. Young people have also been attracted to folk ensembles, the first of which, Karpaty, lasted from 1967 to 1969 under the direction of a recently arrived professional dancer from the Prešov Region in Slovakia, Michael Savčak. In the 1980s, a Karpaty Chorus functioned in Yonkers. Despite these efforts to attract young people, the Lemko Association has become primarily the preserve of first-generation immigrants whose numbers are rapidly decreasing.

A smaller group of Ukrainophile Lemkos felt they have little in common with the policies of the Lemko Association. Led by Mychajlo Dudra and Vasyl' Levčyk, they founded in Philadelphia in 1936 the Organization for the Defense of the Lemko Land (Orhanizacija Oborony Lemkivščyny), which was opposed to the former Polish government's policy of considering Lemkos a nationality distinct from Ukrainians. This group dissolved in 1940, but later revived in Yonkers, New York in 1958 under the leadership of Julijan Nalysnyk. By the 1960s, it claimed 1,500 members, and among its publications which have appeared in literary Ukrainian are *Lemkivs'kyj dzvin* (New York, 1936-40) and *Lemkivs'ki visti* (Yonkers, N.Y. and Toronto, 1958-present). A World Lemkos Federation came into being in 1973, which under the leadership of Ivan Hvozda

attempted, though unsuccessfully, to function as an umbrella organization for all Ukrainian-oriented Lemko groups. The federation has managed to publish five volumes of a scholarly journal, *Annals* (Camillus, N.Y., 1974-91). Finally, in an attempt to consolidate limited resources, these two organizations also support the Lemko Research Foundation in Clifton, New Jersey, which publishes the Ukrainian-language quarterly, *Lemkivščyna* (New York, Clifton, N.J., 1979-present), and in 1982 they all cooperated to open a Lemko Museum as part of the Museum of the Ukrainian Catholic Church in Stamford, Connecticut.

Besides meeting periodically for social and cultural functions, the main activity of these various Ukrainian-oriented Lemko groups seems to be the publication of periodicals and some books (including a recent one on wooden churches) explaining the fate that has befallen their homeland. Most of the members are post-World War II immigrants who experienced first hand the displacement of the Lemko population from its ancestral Carpathian homeland in Galicia eastward to the Soviet Ukraine and westward and northward to other parts of Poland. Consequently, they are adamantly

49. The Phoenixville Falcons, Greek Catholic Union's Sokol baseball team, no. 98 from Phoenixville, Pennsylvania, 1931.

anti-Communist and anti-Polish, as well as Ukrainian in national orientation, factors which not surprisingly make them natural antagonists of the older Lemko Association. Since 1989, the pages of *Lemkivščyna* have also been filled with harsh criticism of the Rusyn national revival in Europe, and this attitude has further alienated pro-Ukrainian Lemkos from the larger Rusyn-American community.

Besides fraternal, cultural, and regional organizations, the Carpatho-Rusyns have also had their own sports and youth organizations. The oldest of these was the Sokol athletic organization of the GCU. Founded in 1910, the Sokol sponsored throughout the northeast United States a broad network of basketball teams and other sports activities. The Sokol also had its own newspaper, the *Amerikansky Russky Sokol* (Homestead, Pa., 1918-36), as well as a youth branch with its own organ, *Svit ditej/Children's World* (Homestead, Pa., 1917-36). These publications contained reports on sports activities and also articles designed to promote awareness of the Old-World culture.

Similarly, the Johnstown Diocese set up in 1937 the American Carpatho-Russian Youth of the Orthodox Greek Catholic Church, whose goals have been to promote social, cultural, and educational development among its approximately 1,000 members. This youth group has also had its own publications, often filled with articles stressing its "Carpathian Russian" heritage: *Carpatho-Russian Youth* (Johnstown, Pa.; Binghamton, N.Y., 1938-41), *ACRY Annual and Church Almanac* (Ligonier, Pa.; Pittsburgh, 1949-present), and the *ACRY Guardian* (New York; Perth Amboy, N.J., 1957-62). For its part, the Byzantine Ruthenian Catholic Church has, since the 1960s, had a Byzantine Catholic Youth Organization. Branches exist at several parishes throughout the country and are concerned primarily with coordinating social functions for children, teenagers, singles, and young married couples. Among the most popular youth organizations are the performing folk groups, which will be discussed more extensively in Chapter 6.

50. The Greek Catholic Union's Sokol Girls' basketball team from Bridgeport, Connecticut, 1930-31.

Chapter 6

Culture

Carpatho-Rusyn culture in the United States has been expressed most naturally through the family unit, sometimes through fraternal organizations, but most especially through the church. Besides basic customs and habits, including language, learned from the family, it is really the religious context that is most important as a cultural identifier. In fact, the role of religion is so great that in the mind of most immigrants and their descendants, Carpatho-Rusyn culture is virtually synonymous with the Eastern-rite liturgy (originally sung in Church Slavonic) and the attendant rituals and family celebrations (births, marriages, funerals) associated with the church.

At the level of the family, it is cuisine and home handicrafts that symbolize most poignantly the "old country" culture. Recipes handed down from grandparents—stuffed cabbage *(holobci/holubki)*, homemade noodles *(halušký)*, stuffed peppers, and the generous use of garlic and sour cream in the preparation of many dishes—as well as embroidered or crocheted needlework and painted Easter eggs *(pysankŷ)* are still integral elements of Carpatho-Rusyn family life even after language and other cultural attributes have been long forgotten. The tradition of painted Easter eggs in their distinct Carpatho-Rusyn forms, which are generally symmetric short-stroke patterns using floral motifs and figures from life or a more geometric line style, has undergone a recent vogue. In some communities, classes have been organized

to teach the skill to Americans of Rusyn and non-Rusyn background alike. The painted eggs and some of the traditional recipes are directly related to the religious calendar. Easter, in particular,

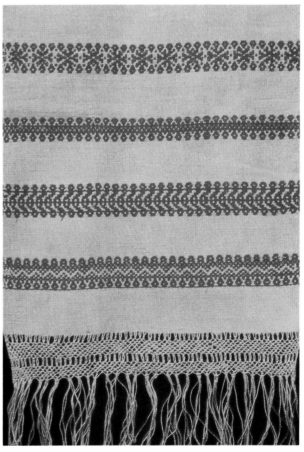

51. Embroidered ritual cloth *(ručnyk)* from the Prešov Region (former Zemplén county) in Czechoslovakia.

52. Rusyn hand-painted Easter eggs in (left) the geometric line style; and (right) the short-stroke pattern with real-life figures (photo by Anton Žižka).

53. Baskets filled with painted eggs (*pysanký*) and covered embroidered ritual cloths at the traditional Easter morning blessing led by Father Alexis Toth outside St. Mary's Church, Minneapolis, Minnesota, *ca.* 1890.

remains a memorable occasion, as the full gamut of Rusyn cuisine is again made available to palates that (if tradition is followed) have been especially whetted because of fasting during the Lenten season.

Even more striking evidence of the close ties between religion and Carpatho-Rusyn culture in America is the most important building outside of the familial home, the church. With regard to church architecture, many of the early structures first in wood and later in stone or brick were modeled on architectural prototypes brought from the homeland. These Old-World models reflected both the eastern and western influences that characterized Carpatho-Rusyn culture in Europe. Thus, while some Rusyn-American churches, especially among the Orthodox, were built according to the central-domed eastern style based on a Greek-cross ground plan, most were constructed on a hybrid pattern. This style meant that their ground plans followed the western, basilica form, having a nave and transept and one or two towers dominating the westwork (western facade). The towers

were often topped with golden, Baroque-style "onion" domes above which were placed three-barred Eastern-rite crosses. Many of these old "Russian" churches, as they are often incorrectly designated, are still standing and remain distinct landmarks in many urban centers of the northeastern United States. The eastern character of these structures was particularly noticeable in the interiors, which usually had icon screens (iconostases) separating the altar from the congregation. Such churches clearly reminded the parishioners of their cultural relations with the Carpatho-Rusyn homeland which, in turn, found its religious and artistic inspiration in Orthodox Byzantium.

At least until World War II, churches built by the Byzantine Ruthenian Catholic and Orthodox communities maintained traditional architectural styles. Since then, however, building costs and changing tastes have led to the construction of more "modern" structures, most often in a bland functional style that hardly distinguishes them externally—and in many cases internally as well—from other Catholic and even Protestant churches.

54. Iconostasis, St. John the Baptist Byzantine Catholic Church, Lyndora, Pennsylvania, crafted by John Baycura, 1915.

55. SS Peter and Paul Greek Catholic Church, Minersville, Pennsylvania, built 1896. An early example of the western-oriented basilica style.

56. St. Theodosius Russian Orthodox Greek Catholic Cathedral, Cleveland, Ohio, 1896. Early example of the eastern-oriented central-domed style.

While construction of these simplistic, nondescript structures has become the rule in recent years, there have nonetheless been a few exceptions. The Byzantine Ruthenian Catholic Church of St. Mary in New York City (lower Manhattan), completed in 1963, combines both the functionalism of the modern international school of architecture with many motifs of the Carpatho-Rusyn Eastern-rite heritage. Another adaptation of architectural tradition is to build entirely in wood, such as the striking Carpathian wooden church constructed for a new Byzantine Ruthenian parish in the Atlanta suburb of Roswell, Georgia.

The early immigrants have left other marks on the American cultural landscape, especially in local graveyards. Several cemeteries in towns where Carpatho-Rusyns settled contain gravestones with the visually distinct Eastern-rite three- or two-barred cross. Aside from the number of bars on the crosses, Rusyn graves are also easy to determine if their inscriptions are written in Cyrillic letters (using Rusyn phonetic transcription) or if they use Hungarian spellings in the Roman alphabet for Slavic names (for instance, Maczko, Zsatkovics).

Music has been a particularly important element in Carpatho-Rusyn culture. Secular music

57. Holy Trinity Russian Orthodox Church, Chicago, Illinois, built 1903. Stylized central-domed style by the leading American architect Louis Sullivan.

in the form of Rusyn folk melodies was most often sung, and in some cases still is, although in a homogenized form at wedding receptions and other family gatherings. Social dancing to spirited Carpathian rhythms like the *karička* (girls' circle dance) and most especially the *čardaš* (the most popular "Rusyn" dance) were widespread during the first decades of this century, although they have been replaced by more "international" and stylized dances like the waltz or, for a more Slavic flavor, the Slovenian polka, the Polish polka, the Russian *kalinka,* and the Ukrainian *kozačok.*

The desire to perform the Old-World dances and songs in their original musical and lyrical form has become the goal of Rusyn-American folk ensembles. While many such groups existed during the earlier years of this century, by the 1950s they had begun to disappear. There was a revival, however, related in large part to the "roots fever" and general interest in ethnicity that swept much of the United States during the mid-1970s. Although often associated with a parish church or fraternal society, these ensembles were usually founded and led by young people interested in learning the dances and in making and donning the colorful

costumes representative of the Carpatho-Rusyn heritage.

Not surprisingly, the new groups were based in the traditional centers of Rusyn-American settlement—the metropolitan areas of Pittsburgh, Cleveland, and Detroit. Often organized for several age levels and encouraging parent participation, the folk ensembles showed a real potential to draw and to maintain interest in popular Carpatho-Rusyn culture. Among the most effective activists in the folk ensemble movement during the 1970s and 1980s was Jerry Jumba, a professional musician and choreographer, who initiated and/or participated in many of the dozen new ensembles that came into being. Among these were the Carpathian Youth Choir and Dancers (Monessen, Pennsylvania), Rusynŷ (McKeesport, Pennsylvania), Karpaty (Ambridge, Pennsylvania), Kruzhok (Parma, Ohio),

58. Rusyn tombstones at the Rose Hill Cemetary (left), Butler, Pennsylvania (photo by Peter Bajcura) and the Lower Cemetary (right), Proctor, Vermont (photo by Paul Robert Magocsi).

Beskidy Rusyns (Livonia, Michigan), Krajane (Sterling Heights, Michigan), and the Carpathians (Barberton, Ohio). By the late 1980s, however, most of these groups ceased functioning, either because the initial enthusiasm of the "roots fever" years had worn off, or because they were unable to find financial support from the established religious and secular organizations which, in general, remained unmoved by the ethnic revival. As a result, today only four of the groups founded since 1975 are still active—Slavjane (McKees Rocks, Pennsylvania), the Holy Ghost Choir and Dancers (Philadelphia, Pennsylvania), the Carpathians (Binghamton, New York), and the St. Michael's Youth Folk Dance Group (Chicago, Illinois).

While interest in secular music performed by Rusyn-American folk ensembles has risen and fallen at various times, church music has been more constant. The dominant feature of the church repertoire is the *prostopinije,* or liturgical plain chant, which is still used in both Byzantine Catholic and Orthodox churches. The *prostopinije* brought by the early immigrants from the Carpatho-Rusyn homeland was distinct from other Eastern-rite chant music because it incorporated numerous local folk melodies. This specific liturgical music has been preserved by generations of church choirs as well as by more formal programs, such as cantors' schools and the Carpatho-Rusyn Liturgical Chant Renewal Program run by Jerry Jumba for the Byzantine Ruthenian Metropolitan Archdiocese of Pittsburgh between 1984 and 1992.

Several choirs have also produced records with both religious and secular folk music, including renditions of the spirited Carpatho-Rusyn national anthem, "Podkarpatskij rusynŷ, ostavte hlubokyj son" (Subcarpathian Rusyns, Arise From Your Deep Slumber), and the even more popular "Ja rusyn bŷl, jesm' i budu" (I Was, Am, and Will

59. Carpatho-Russian Orthodox Greek Catholic Church of St. John the Baptist, Mill Hill Avenue, Bridgeport, Connecticut, built 1946, by architect Jesse J. Hamblin. Neo-Byzantine basilica and central-domed hybrid modelled after the Church of Madeleine in Paris.

60. St. Mary Byzantine Catholic Church, 15th Street and Second Avenue, Manhattan, New York City, built 1963, by architect Cajetan J.B. Baumann, OFM.

61. Epiphany Byzantine Catholic Church, Roswell, Georgia, built 1982, by architect James Barker. Stylized traditional Carpathian wooden church (photo by Jim Frankenburger).

62. Holy Trinity Orthodox Church, Wilkeson, Washington, typical clapboard rural church (photo by Orestes Mihaly).

Remain a Rusyn). Particularly well represented over the past three decades, with several recordings to their credit, are the Holy Ghost Byzantine Choir of Philadelphia, directed by Daniel J. Kavka; St. Mary's Metropolitan Choir of New York City, directed by Gabriel Zihal; and the St. Mary Choir of Van Nuys, California, directed by Michael M. Bodnar—all associated with the Byzantine Ruthenian Catholic Church; Christ the Saviour Cathedral Choir of Johnstown, Pennsylvania, directed by Andrew Panchisin, and St. Michael's Church Choir of Binghamton, New York, directed by Edward

Sedor—both with the Johnstown Diocese; and St. John the Baptist Russian Orthodox Church Choir of Passaic, New Jersey, directed by Michael Hilko, of the Orthodox Church in America (OCA).

The combination of music, spiritual devotion, and an appropriate architectural and natural setting is also expressed among those Carpatho-Rusyns in the United States who still actively maintain the Old-World custom of annual religious processions and retreats known as *otpusti*. These events are usually associated with retreats, such as those held at St. Tikhon's Monastery outside of Scranton, Pennsylvania among Orthodox in the OCA; at Holy Trinity Monastery in Jordanville, New York among the Orthodox in the Synod; at Christ the Saviour Seminary in Johnstown, Pennsylvania and at the Annunciation Monastery in Tuxedo Park, New York for Orthodox in the Johnstown Diocese; and at the Monastery of the Basilian Fathers of Mariapoch in Matawan, New Jersey among Byzantine Ruthenian Catholics.

The oldest and largest of these religious processions/retreats is held each August on the grounds of the Basilian Convent at Mount St.

Macrina near Uniontown, Pennsylvania, south of Pittsburgh. Each Labor Day weekend since 1934, as many as 40,000 Byzantine Ruthenian Catholics have gathered to renew their faith, and by so doing to re-emphasize a sense of community among the group's members. The sisters at Mt. Macrina, in addition, have published for many years a periodical, *The Voice of Mount St. Macrina/Holos Hory Sv. Makriny* (Uniontown, Pa., 1948-present), which especially in its early years contained material on Carpatho-Rusyn culture. In 1975, during the height of the "roots fever" in America, the Basilian sisters sponsored a two-day cultural seminar on Carpathian Rus', which brought together secular and clerical scholars to lecture on several aspects of Rusyn history, language, and culture.

Another Old-World tradition that was begun and is still maintained among Carpatho-Rusyns in the United States is a celebration known as Rusyn Day *(Rus'kyj Den')*, held during the summer months and often at amusement parks. Rusyn Days have been geared to both people of Carpatho-Rusyn background as well as to the larger American public. Traditionally, the annual event includes speeches by Carpatho-Rusyn religious and secular leaders (joined sometimes by local politicians) as well as performances by folk choirs and dance groups. The oldest Rusyn Day cele-

bration has been held since 1921 at Kennywood Park in Pittsburgh. From the 1920s until the 1950s, several towns in the northeast had annual Rusyn days, among the largest being those at Luna Park in Cleveland and at Idora Park in Youngstown, Ohio. Since 1969, the Lemkos have held annual "Carpatho-Russian" festivals at their resort in Monroe, New York.

Among the various cultural characteristics associated with ethnic groups, language frequently has been considered the most important vehicle for transmitting and preserving group identity. With regard to language as a carrier of Carpatho-Rusyn culture in the United States, it would be useful first to emphasize the differences that exist between spoken and written languages. All languages are composed of several spoken dialects and one, or even more than one, standard written form. Moreover, there is often a substantial difference between the standard written form of a language and the dialects that the written form ostensibly represents.

In the European homeland, Carpatho-Rusyns, at the time of the largest migration to America before World War I, communicated in a variety of speech which belonged to either the Prešov Region, Lemko Region, or Transcarpathian (Subcarpathian) dialectal groups, all of which have

63. Slavjane Folk Ensemble, McKees Rocks, Pennsylvania.

64. Carpathian Youth Choir and Dancers, Monessen, Pennsylvania (photo by George W. Shusta).

65. Otpust-religious procession at Mount St. Macrina, Uniontown, Pennsylvania, 1968.

66. Clergy lead the festivities on Rusyn Day (*Rus'kyj Den'*), Olympia Park, Cleveland, July 16, 1935.

The 34th Annual
RUSIN DAY

Sponsored by
THE RUSIN DAY ASSOCIATION OF GREATER CLEVELAND, INC.

S U N D A Y
July 26, 1959

ST. JOHN'S GROVE
5822 BROADVIEW ROAD
PARMA, OHIO

REV. MYRON HORVATH, CHAIRMAN
RUSIN DAY COMMITTEE

PROCEEDS FOR BENEFIT OF THE
CLEVELAND BYZANTINE RITE DEANERY

67. Program to the annual Rusyn Day in the Cleveland area.

been classified by modern linguists as part of the Ukrainian language. However, living along the extreme western portion of the Ukrainian linguistic area, the Carpatho-Rusyns were strongly influenced by the Slovak, Polish, and Hungarian languages. The immigrants described their native speech in a variety of ways: (1) Rusyn *(rus'kyj)*, which in English was frequently and incorrectly rendered as Russian or Carpatho-Russian; (2) "Slavish," a meaningless term which probably arose as a result of sharing with eastern Slovak dialect speakers many terms and expressions; and (3) *po-našomu,* meaning in our own way.

Despite what the immigrants actually spoke—various Rusyn dialects—and notwithstanding what they called their language, they also wrote and published in a wide variety of linguistic forms and alphabets. An analysis of their publications has revealed that basically three types of written languages were used. These may be classified as: (1) the Subcarpathian dialectal variant; (2) the Lemko dialectal variant; and (3) the Carpatho-Rusyn recension (variant) of Russian.

The Subcarpathian variant reflected the spoken language of immigrants from the Prešov Region of present-day northeastern Slovakia (sometimes with strong East Slovak dialectal influences) and from the Transcarpathian oblast in Ukraine (Transcarpathian dialects). This was the form used in the most widely read newspapers, such as the *Amerikansky russky viestnik* (1892-1952), *Prosvita* (1917-present), *Vostok* (1919-50), *Russkij vistnik* (1917-present), and the only daily, *Den'* (1922-27). Some of these publications originally used the Cyrillic alphabet (including the old orthography distinguished by the letters ъ and ы),but by the 1930s they changed to a Czech-based Latin alphabet (recognizable by use of the *haček* accent over certain letters—č=ch, š=sh, ž=zh—as well as apostrophes to indicate East Slavic soft signs usually at the end of words).

The Lemko variant reflected the spoken language of Lemkos from Galicia and was used in most publications of the Lemko Association, such as *Karpatska Rus'* (1938-present), which still uses the Cyrillic alphabet in its modern orthography. The third written form, the Carpatho-Rusyn recension of Russian, represented the attempt of some Carpatho-Rusyn immigrants from various regions to write in Russian. The result was an unstandardized language using the Cyrillic alphabet (in the old orthography) that tried to follow the rudiments of literary Russian grammar

---

(1)

VAŠICH RUKACH, dorohoj čitateľ, jubilejnyj vypusk našeho officiaľnoho organa "Vostoka", s uveličennym količestvom stranic.

Jubilejnyj nomer! Jubilej dvadcať pjať ľitňaho sušćestvovanija odnoj iz nemnohich karpatorusskich zapomohovych organizacij v Sojedinennych Štatach — organizacii Svobody.

Dľa postoronnaho čitateľa sej jubilejnyj nomer ne označajet inšoho, jak uveličennoje količestvo stranic: bohato dobranyj material, snimki, stat'ji iz pod pera raznych lic, mnoho pozdravitel'nych i kommerčeskich privitstvij i proč. No dľa členov-truženikov sej jubilej označajet zaveršenije dvadcať pjať ľitnaho truda na organizacijnym poprišći.

Každyj jubilej — eto obzor vseho toho, čto bylo sd'ilano za minuvšij srok. I tak, jak v nastojašćem mjsjaci my stavim točku v konci toj raboty, kotoru my končili v proť'aženii četvert' stoľitija, ne budet neumistnym ohľanutis' nazad na projdennyj nami puť i dati sebi otčet iz našich dostiženij.

Neotricajemyj fakt, čto my za dvadcať pjať ľit krasnu rabotu zrobili. Naše členstvo — v tysjaćech. Vopreki tomu, čto u nas ňit organizacijnych znatokov-ekspertov, jak u druhich velikich inorodnych zapomohovych organizacijach, kotory rukovoďat organizacijnymi d'ilami, my sumili sozdati organizaciju, kotora po svojemu dostojinstvu možet zanimati odno iz pervych mist sredi karpatorusskich zapomohovych organizacij.

Vostok, July 1943.

(2)

V New Yorku byla deržana konferencia meždu kompaniami mjahkoho uhľa i zastupnikami majnerskej unii. Na začatku konferencii tak pokazovalosja, že iz toho nebude cilkom nič, poneže kompanie nijak nechotili pristati na sije, čtoby ot 1-ho april'a 1923, pod takima uslovijami byli majnery platene, jak teper polučajut za svoju robotu, a to dľa klevlandskej konferencii rišenija. Konečno po dlukšom razbiraniju majnerskoho voprosa, na vlijanije pravitelstva iz Washingtonu, kompanie prijmajut to, že podpišu paktum klevelandskej konferencii na odin rok. (To jest, ot 1-ho april'a 1923, do 1-ho april'a 1924. Zastupniki majnerskej unii chotili na dva roki, no to neudalosja. Tak samo i to bylo prijato ne newyorskej konferencii, že načalom roku 1924 poderži sja znova taka konferencia, aby bylo obkerpovano strajku ot 1-ho april'a 1924.

Slava Tebi Hospodi! — Choťaj odno važnoje d'ilo pokojno rišeno i majnery budut spokojno prodolžati svoju robotu do 1-ho april'a 1924. hoda. Sija radostnaja sprava ne toľko pro majnerov, no i pro každoho obchodnika i urjadnika.

Russkij viestnik, January 25, 1923.

(3)

Посылаю вам сердечне поздоровлення и желаю всім робочым при газеті, чытателям и дописователям газеты, котри роблят нашу газету интересантнійшом, найлучшого здоровя.

"Карпатска Русь", яка пишеся нашым народным говором, чым одрижняеся од другых газет, интересна и тым, што новостями, якы передае, дае нам можливость легше порозуміти значене сьвітовых родин. Чытаючи нашу газету стае ясным, што ничого доброго народа сьвіта не можут сподиватися од тых, што выдаляют билиюны и билиюны доларив на вооружене бо се означае убийство бідного, невинного народа. Се ...

робится тоді, коли инша не загоилися рани нашеі першоі світовоі войны, а про жертвы другоі світовоі войны нихто нам не говорю, бо они свіжи в нашой памяти и очевидни, если оглядите ветеранські шпиталі.

В першой світовой войні я был арестованный з небольшком тактом, об. як и наши покойны предкы, мы голосилися до русской народности, мы остались вірными сынами и дочками нашой православной віры и нашых звычайов. Батько стался жертвою переслідований врагами нашого народа. Умер от мук в Талергофі и там был похованый под соснами.

Karpatska Rus', July 6, 1980.

(4)

Въ попередномъ чисьлѣ высказали мы нашу радость и многольѣтіе тѣмъ членамъ-организаторамъ О. Р. Б., акіи честно трудится надъ организаціею и заохочаютъ легковажныхъ работниковъ, щобы обезпечились, бо ніхто съ насъ не знае коли прійдеся ему перенестись въ вѣчность. — Писали мы и о томъ, що именно членамъ-организаторамъ мають благодарити тѣ вдовы и сироты, що получають запомоги съ организаціи, бо если бы организаторъ, то и половина вдовъ и сиротъ не получили бы запомоги по своихъ отцахъ и мужахъ.

Що тамъ дѣйстно есть, тое може ствердити поимянный выказъ при концѣ минувшого года 14 померлыхъ членовъ. Померли: Іоаннъ Гренко, членъ ч. 1, — Марія Адамьцьо, ч. 4, — Мих. Михалькевичъ, ч. 17. — Теодоръ Малиняакъ и Іосифъ Кафка, ч. 19, — Мих. Письо, ч. 20, — Стефанъ Зиничъ, ч. 28, — Георгій Бованикевичъ, ч. 43, — Іоаннъ Гниданичъ, ч. 63, — Іоаннъ Цимбалакъ, ч. 83, — Алексѣй Томашевскій, ч. 100. — Андрей Гаврила, ч. 100 — и Михаилъ Плешинскій, ч. 126.)

Pravda, February 16, 1923.

---

68. Varieties of Carpatho-Rusyn written languages from the press. (1) *Vostok*—Subcarpathian dialect using the Latin alphabet; (2) *Russkij viestnik*—Subcarpathian dialect using the Cyrillic alphabet; (3) *Karpatska Rus'*—Lemko dialect; (4) *Pravda*—attempts to write in Russian.

but which invariably included numerous lexical and syntactical borrowings from Carpatho-Rusyn dialects. This linguistic form dominated the early years of the newspapers *Svit* (1894-present) and *Pravda* (1902-present), and more recently appeared in the Cyrillic sections of *Carpatho-Russian Echoes/Karpatorusskije otzvuki* (1983-89).

To these three categories of Carpatho-Rusyn written language in the United States were added standard literary Ukrainian *(Karpats'ka zorja, Vistnyk)* and literary Russian *(Pravoslavnaja Rus', Svobodnoe slovo Karpatskoj Rusi)* used by post-World War II immigrants of the Ukrainian or Russian national orientations. But it is English which by far has become the most important language. Today, very few Carpatho-Rusyn immigrants or their descendants speak a language other than English in their daily lives and, with the exception of the Lemko Association newspaper *(Karpatska Rus')* and the now rare Rusyn columns in a few other newspapers *(Church Messenger, Orthodox Herald),* the group's religious and secular press is in English.

Even before English became the dominant linguistic form in the late 1950s and 1960s, it infiltrated Carpatho-Rusyn, so that both the spoken language as well as all three forms of written language rapidly acquired a high number of borrowings from English. This was particularly the case for words related to industrial and political situations not present in the old country at the time of the immigrant's departure. Among the more commonly used examples were *bos* (boss), *kara* (car), *majna* (mine), *burder* (boarder), and *salun* (saloon). English loan-words also quickly entered everyday Carpatho-Rusyn speech—for example, *boysik* (boy), *štor* (store), *porč* (porch), *šusy* (shoes)—so that most first-generation immigrants and their offspring (if they retained their original language at all) spoke at best a kind of Rusyn/English hybrid. Today, the middle and retirement age children of the first immigrants may understand Carpatho-Rusyn, but they are unable to speak very much. The third-, fourth-, and fifth-generation descendants rarely know any Rusyn.

In the past, a few immigrant writers tried to provide some standards for their language. A grammar (1919) and a reader (1919, 1935), both by Father Joseph Hanulya, and three primers

Dorohaya Marushka:

I guess ze ti dumala ze ya leave-vovala svit jak ja nye pisala sooner. Ale ja bula taka busy sos holidays, i ja mala mali mishap zhe ja neznala chi ja coming or going.

Tam tyi Thursday noch, ja bula babysitting, everything ishlo O.K., yak ja noticesovala zhe baby chokuje. Ja dostala so excited, ja grabuvala babu, i turnovala kid upside down, i trepem, i trepem, a ona estche chokuje.

Ja po callovala doctors, on prishol, i powil zati do hospitalya na X-rayse. X-rays buli O.K., i ya vzala jeh domy. Ja bula taka happy zhe nich ne yest wrong, i na druhu ruku taka mad zhe ona scareovala mene.

Ja learnovala taki lesson zhe never zabudem. Ja nihda budem watchovati kidsy anymore. Moji babysitting days pishle het.

Budte zdorovi, Helena

69. Rusyn-English pidgin language as used in an amusing article from the *Orthodox Herald*.

(bukvary) by Peter J. Maczkov (1921), Dmitry Vislocky (1931), and Stefan F. Telep (1938) all strove to provide "literary" forms which could be used in schools and by editors in their publications. In effect, each of these amateur linguists, who knew well only their own Carpatho-Rusyn dialects, tried to write in Russian, the result being highly individual varieties of the Carpatho-Rusyn recension of Russian. It is also interesting to note, that with the exception of Telep, these same authors did not try to write in Russian in their other publications, but rather used the Subcarpathian (Hanulya, Maczkov) or Lemko (Vislocky) Carpatho-Rusyn dialectal variants. Since World War II, there have been a few attempts to provide Carpatho-Rusyn texts for people who want to relearn or learn for the first time the language of their forefathers. The most recent of these are the

two English-Rusyn phrasebooks by Paul R. Magocsi, *Let's Speak Rusyn* (*Bisidujme po-rus'kŷ,* 1976, 1978 and *Hovorim po-rus'kŷ,* 1979), based on the speech of individual villages in the Prešov Region and the Transcarpathian oblast.

In the end, spoken Carpatho-Rusyn has not survived, because there have been few formal means for preserving it. During the 1940s and 1950s, radio stations in cities like New York, Pittsburgh, and Cleveland offered short programs in Carpatho-Rusyn, and until the early 1960s most priests still gave brief homilies in the language, although the liturgy was sung in Church Slavonic, a classical language that functioned as Latin did until the 1960s in the Roman Catholic Church. But today English is the predominant language in the Byzantine Ruthenian Catholic and Orthodox churches,

except in some parishes where Church Slavonic may still be used for the liturgy and Rusyn for homilies. Despite its otherwise general decline, Carpatho-Rusyn is still used for the homily on the popular weekly radio church services broadcast for the past three decades from Pittsburgh by the "Byzantine Catholic Radio Bishop" John Bilock.

To be sure, there were educational facilities in Carpatho-Rusyn communities already during the last decade of the nineteenth century. These were usually "ethnic schools," called the *Rus'ka škola* (Rusyn school), that began first in church basements and then later had their own buildings beside or near the church. These early "schools" were actually classes held after the public school day was over, and they were staffed more often than not by church cantors, who, because of their

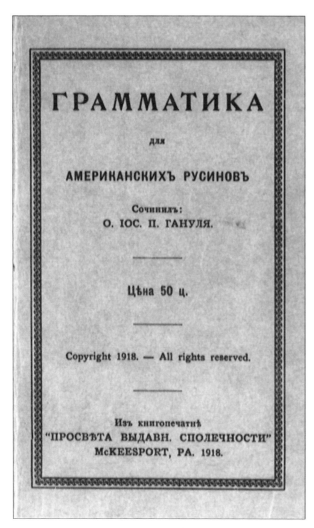

70. Title page of the first grammar for American Rusyns, *Hrammatyka dlja amerykanskych rusynov*, by Father Joseph Hanulya.

71. Title page of a primer for American Lemkos, *Karpatorusskij bukvar'*, by Vanja Hunjanka (pseudonym of Dmitry Vislocky).

72. St. John's Greek Catholic School, Perth Amboy, New Jersey, erected 1921.

activity, popularly became known as "professors." By the 1940s, many of the after-public-school-classes were discontinued, while churches began to sponsor all-day parochial schools staffed, at least in the Byzantine Ruthenian Church, by sisters from the Order of St. Basil the Great. Although the Rusyn religious tradition was still stressed, language and other elements of the Old-World heritage were dropped from the curriculum.

Even during the early decades, when Carpatho-Rusyn language instruction was still offered, there were never any adequate textbooks nor, as we have seen, a clear decision as to what language should be taught—Rusyn vernacular, Russian, or a transitional East Slovak/Rusyn dialect (the so-called Sotak). On the other hand, Carpatho-Rusyn had (and in some cases still has) a functional use in churches—whether in homilies, confessions, or general pastoral work—so that new priests assigned to older "ethnic" parishes are still expected to have some linguistic knowledge in order to communicate with the albeit ever-dwindling numbers of first-generation immigrants. Thus, since the 1950s, both the Byzantine Ruthenian Catholic Seminary in Pittsburgh and the Carpatho-Russian Orthodox Greek Catholic Seminary in Johnstown, Pennsylvania have offered instruction in Carpatho-Rusyn from time to time, but this, too, has been largely ineffectual because of the lack of suitable texts and the restricted use of the language outside the classroom. For the

Orthodox seminary course, a "Carpatho-Russian" text was prepared by Monsignor John Yurcisin, while for the Byzantine Catholic seminary course —offered during the mid-1970s in conjunction with Duquesne University and renewed in the 1990s—a "Ruthenian" text was prepared by Father Athanasius Pekar. Neither of these instructional manuals has yet been published.

The Carpatho-Rusyn immigration has produced a small corpus of belles-lettres. Short plays and collections of poetry were the most popular literary media. Plays describing village life in Europe or the American experience were particularly important, because they provided a repertoire for the adult and children's dramatic circles that before World War II were found in most local parishes and fraternal lodges. The most talented and prolific writer was Father Emilij A. Kubek, who published numerous short stories, poems, and the only novel produced in the Carpatho-Rusyn immigration: *Marko Šoltys: roman iz žit'ja Podkarpatskoj Rusi* (Marko Šoltys: A Novel About Life in Subcarpathian Rus', 1923), 3 volumes. Three other capable writers whose literary careers began in Europe but who also published in the United States were Dmitry Vislocky, author of short stories and plays in the Lemko dialect about life in the immigration and the homeland—*V Ameryki* (In

73. Father Emilij A. Kubek.

74. Cast of the *Bereg Wedding* (*Berecka svad'ba*), performance in 1935 by the parishioners of the St. John the Baptist Church, Perth Amboy, New Jersey.

America, 1932), *Šoltys* (1938), *Petro Pavlyk* (1937); the Russian-oriented Dmitry Vergun—*Karpatorusskie otzvuki* (Carpatho-Russian Echoes, 1920), and the Ukrainian-language lyric poet, and Basilian monk, Sevastijan Sabol, pseudonym Zoreslav—*Z rannich vesen* (From Early Spring, 1963).

The remaining belletrists were amateurs, whose work had more sentimental, patriotic, and linguistic significance than any literary value. Among the more popular writers were Peter P. Hatalak, Peter J. Maczkov, Stefan F. Telep, and several priests: Sigmund Brinsky, Valentine Gorzo, Orestes Koman, Ivan A. Ladižinsky, Jurion Thegze, and Stefan Varzaly.

A few belletrists of second-generation Carpatho-Rusyn background used autobiographical elements in some of their English-language works. The most well-known of these was the novelist and dramatist, Thomas Bell, whose father came from the Prešov Region in northeastern Slovakia. Several of his novels dealt with the fate of

Rusyn, Slovak, and other east-central European immigrants during the Great Depression. The best known of these was *Out of This Furnace* (1941). The hardships of the 1930s also served as the backdrop for the novel, *Icon of Spring* (1987), by Sonya Jason, the daughter of immigrants from Subcarpathian Rus' who continues to incorporate Rusyn-American themes in her writings.

More widely read than belles-lettres was the large variety of polemical pamphlet literature. In a community that was continually rent by religious, political, and national controversy, it is not surprising that attacks and counterattacks were often the "literary" order of the day. And the environment was almost always one in which subtlety and persuasion by nuance were virtually unknown. Instead, blunt and aggressive, though in retrospect colorful titles often summed up the "objective" and "truthful" arguments put forth by the avid polemicists. Typical in this genre for religious argumentation were pamphlets like: *Where to Seek the Truth* (1894) by Father Alexis Toth; *Whose Truth*

NARODNY POVISTI I STICHI.

MARKO ŠOLTYS

ROMAN IZ ŽIT'JA PODKARPATSKOJ RUSI.

NAPISAL: EMILIJ A. KUBEK.

———

ILLUSTROVAL: ANTONIJ E. KUBEK.

———

II. TOM (VOLUME)

75. Title page of the novel *Marko Šoltys* by Emilij A. Kubek.

Is It? That of the Catholics or Non-Catholics?! (1922) by Father Joseph P. Hanulya; *Joan the Woman Pope* (193?) by Father John J. Hriecenak; *Why Am I a Greek Catholic of the Orthodox Faith?* (1939) by Father Peter J. Molchany; or *Should a Priest Be Married?* (1942) by Father Joseph Mihaly. The defense of "Rusynism" through anti-Czechoslovak or anti-Ukrainian attacks was most evident in politicized tracts like: *Wilson's Principles in Czechoslovak Practice: The Situation of the Czechoslovak People Under the Czech Yoke* (1929) by Michael Yuhasz, or *The Biggest Lie of the Century—'the Ukraine'* (1952) and *Highlights of Russian History and the 'Ukrainian' Provocation (1955)*, both by Father Peter G. Kohanik.

The largest percentage of Carpatho-Rusyn belles-lettres, polemical articles, and more serious historical and social commentaries did not come

out as separate titles, but rather appeared in the more than 60 newspapers and annual almanacs that have been printed since 1892 and have been published for the most part by the community's several churches and fraternal organizations. There was even a large format, though short-lived Rusyn-American literary monthly called *Niva* (Yonkers, N.Y., 1916).

Many of the individual titles were put out before the 1950s by publishing houses such as the Greek Catholic Union Typography (Homestead, Pennsylvania), the Vostok and Vestal Publishing Company (Perth Amboy, New Jersey), and George Sabo (Pearl River, New York). The problem of distribution during these early years was handled by bookdealers like Julius Egreczky of Cleveland, John Korman of Braddock, Pennsylvania, and George Sabo of Pearl River, New York and later Melbourne, Florida. The financial requirements of these businessmen were complemented by a sense of patriotism that prompted them to diffuse knowledge of Carpatho-Rusyn culture both within

76. Title page of the Rusyn-American literary and religious monthly, *Niva*, eleven issues (352 pages) of which appeared in 1916.

and beyond the community. With the changeover to English during the last three decades, two new publishing houses have come into existence: the Byzantine Seminary Press (Pittsburgh, Pennsylvania) publishes mostly religious-related materials, while the Carpatho-Rusyn Research Center (Fairview, New Jersey) is concerned primarily with works about the secular as well as religious heritage of the group both in Europe and in the United States.

The world of scholarship and the arts has also been enriched by a few Carpatho-Rusyn immigrants and their descendants. The history of the group itself in both Europe and America has quite naturally become the focus of attention. Several learned priests, in particular, have tried their hand

77. Title page of the *Carpatho-Rusyn American*, published quarterly since 1978 by the Carpatho-Rusyn Research Center.

at providing historical accounts of various aspects of Carpatho-Rusyn culture. Among the earliest was Father Joseph P. Hanulya, who wrote the first history in English of *Rusin Literature* (1941). He has been followed by several other Byzantine Catholic priests, all of whom have written on some aspect of Carpatho-Rusyn religious history: Stephen C. Gulovich, Julius Kubinyi, Basil Boysak, John Slivka, and among the most prolific, Basil Shereghy, Athanasius Pekar, and in Canada, Alexander Baran.

There have also been a few self-trained laymen who have chronicled certain aspects of Carpatho-Rusyn history. These include Simeon Pysh and Dmitry Vislocky, who wrote on the Lemko Region; Augustine Stefan and Vincent Shandor, who have been concerned primarily with the era of Carpatho-Ukrainian autonomy (1938-1939); and Michael Roman, who has prepared popular literature on the European heritage and life in America.

Beyond the perimeters of the community are several scholars of Carpatho-Rusyn background who have made their mark in American universities and research centers. Among these are: the physicist Oleksa M. Bilaniuk, Swarthmore College; the geographer George J. Demko, Dartmouth University; the historian Basil Dmytryshyn, Portland State University; the electrical engineer Nick Holonyak, University of Illinois; the Slavic bibliographer Edward Kasinec, New York Public Library; the Hindi linguist Colin S. Masica, University of Chicago; the astrophysicist Andrew Skumanich, National Center for Atmospheric Research; and the linguist Michael Zarechnak, Georgetown University. Several other university scholars of Carpatho-Rusyn background, especially in the humanities and social sciences, have published studies about their ancestral heritage: Patricia Krafcik, Evergreen State College; Paul R. Magocsi, University of Toronto; Vasyl Markus, Loyola University; Richard Renoff, City University of New York; John Reshetar, University of Washington; Elaine Rusinko, University of Maryland; and Peter G. Stercho, Drexel University.

There are also a few descendants of Carpatho-Rusyn immigrants who have made successful careers in the world of American art and entertainment. The eminent choral director and arranger Peter J. Wilhousky began his singing in the choir of a Carpatho-Rusyn parish in Passaic, New

78. Sandra Dee.

famous paintings of *Two Hundred Campbell's Soup Cans* (1962) and *Brillo Boxes* (1964), and then he shocked the underground film world with his award-winning—though often long and boring—motion pictures such as *Eat* (1963), *Chelsea Girls* (1966), and *Trash* (1971).

Despite Andy Warhol's fame in the world of contemporary American art and film, there is another person of Carpatho-Rusyn background whose otherwise anonymous image is known to almost every American. He is Michael Strank, a Rusyn immigrant from the Prešov Region and later a sergeant in the United States Marine Corps. Strank was one of the six marines who raised the American flag atop a rugged mountain on Iwo Jima during the bitter battle against the Japanese for control of that Pacific Ocean island toward the end of World War II. Although killed in action within a week after the flag-raising (February 23,

Jersey. He became best known for the now classic arrangements of the Yuletide "Carol of the Bells" and the stirring "Battle Hymn of the Republic" immortalized in recordings by the Morman Tabernacle Choir. Still active is Richard Dufallo, program director at the Julliard School of Music (New York City) and at the Aspen Music Festival in Colorado, who credits his predilection for Slavic classical music to his "Subcarpathian Ruthenian background."

Among other performers to achieve national success are a few Hollywood film stars. Lizabeth Scott (born Emma Matzo), the daughter of Carpatho-Rusyn immigrants from Subcarpathian Rus', played the role of a sultry leading lady in several films during the late 1940s and early 1950s. Somewhat later, Sandra Dee (born Alexandra Zuk), the granddaughter of Lemko immigrants, starred in roles as the prototypical American teenage girl in several Hollywood films of the early 1960s. More recently, Robert Urich, who is of mixed Rusyn-Slovak origin, starred during the 1980s in a popular television series and has since made several movies. But by far the most famous descendant of Carpatho-Rusyn immigrants (both parents were from a Rusyn village in the Prešov Region of northeastern Slovakia) was Andy Warhol, the artist, photographer, and filmmaker, raised during the depression in Pittsburgh's *Ruska dolina* (Rusyn valley). This "enfant terrible" of the 1960s rocked the world of Pop Art with his

79. Andy Warhol, *200 Campbell's Soup Cans*, 1962, one of several versions of this painting that, in the words of one critic, "made Warhol's name almost as familiar as Campbell's."

1945), Strank was posthumously awarded numerous military decorations. He subsequently was immortalized because the wartime photograph of the flag raising was later transformed into the famous "Iwo Jima Monument" just outside Washington, D.C., symbolizing American bravery during the last world conflict.

Finally, Carpatho-Rusyns and specifically their cultural experience in America have been the subject of attention in at least two works written by authors from outside the group. During the 1930s, the most outstanding twentieth-century Czech author, Karel Čapek, wrote a novel, *Hordubal* (1934), which analyzed the psychological and familial difficulties faced by a Carpatho-Rusyn immigrant who returned home to his native village after working several years in Pennsylvania.

More recently, the American script-writer E. M. Corder based a tale, *The Deerhunter* (1978), on a group of Rusyn Americans from Clairton, Pennsylvania, whose lives were brutally disrupted by the Vietnam War, in which several were wounded or died in particularly unpleasant circumstances. The Carpatho-Rusyns were used to typify those many elements in the United States who, despite the numerous protests engendered by the war, served voluntarily and remained patriotic Americans even after their personal lives were so horribly damaged. *The Deerhunter* received national acclaim as an academy-award winning film, and although the term Carpatho-Rusyn is never used in the film (Russian is), the marriage scene was shot in St. Theodosius Orthodox Cathedral and the wedding reception *(hostyna)* in the Lemko Hall (both in Cleveland and with "locals" who uttered a few words in Rusyn dialect), so that the setting, dialogue, and action of the participants leave no doubt that the film is a contemporary saga about Americans of Slavic and more precisely Carpatho-Rusyn background.

80. United States commemorative postage stamp of the Iwo Jima Monument issued in 1945. Michael Strank is third from the left (under the upraised arm).

Chapter 7

Politics

For Carpatho-Rusyn immigrants and their descendants, politics has had a special connotation. It has not meant participation in the American political system, but rather a pervasive concern with the fate of the homeland, endless debates about the problem of ethnic or national self-identity, and considerable interaction with other ethnic groups of similar geographic background in the United States.

There were at least two reasons why the early Carpatho-Rusyn immigrants were reluctant to become involved in American political life. First of all, many of the newcomers thought they had come to the United States on a temporary basis, and therefore they had neither the time nor interest, let alone the linguistic skills or political experience, to take part in "American" matters. In fact, their only real experience in the American political process came as strikers (or sometimes hired strike-breakers) in the labor disturbances that often rocked the industrial centers they inhabited. Nonetheless, it should be pointed out that Carpatho-Rusyns were never singled out as a group, but rather castigated for their activity or tolerated for their existence along with their fellow eastern European immigrant workers, all of whom were lumped together under the opprobrious terms, *Hunkies* or *Polaks*.

Even when it was clear that their permanent home really was to be the United States, the Old-World experience with politics in which the fate of Carpatho-Rusyns was usually decided by others led many of them to maintain a negative and pessimistic view of the political process. Their own newspapers and almanacs, which frequently featured success stories about political activists and national heroes like President Washington and Lincoln, seemed to have little real impact. For the longest time it was not possible to find a Carpatho-Rusyn name on a list of local, state, or national elected officials.

There were a few attempts during the late 1930s and 1940s to enlist Carpatho-Rusyns to vote as a bloc in American political life, especially in the northeast where most lived. Although there was a Carpatho-Russian division in the Republican party in Pennsylvania, it was the Democratic party that attracted most members of the group. An American Rusin Democratic League and a Democratic Club headed by attorney Sigmund T. Brinsky functioned for a while in Ohio, while in New York a Carpatho-Russian division of the Democratic party was formed as early as 1932. Headed by businessman Michael Mahonic, the New York division claimed to be national in scope, but in practice it was limited to that state and to nearby Connecticut, where until the early 1950s it did help to elect local candidates on the Democratic ticket.

In general, however, the community never had any real impact on American politics and no politicians have ever talked about a Carpatho-Rusyn bloc of votes. Only since the 1970s have there been a few elected and appointed officials of Carpatho-Rusyn background: Mark Singel, lieutenant governor of Pennsylvania; Orestes Mihaly, assistant attorney general of New York;

Congressman Joseph M. Gaydos, Democrat from Pennsylvania; Judge Richard Zeleznik, Allegheny County, Pennsylvania; and federal civil servants especially in the Department of State: George J. Demko, geographer; and Dimitry Zarechnak, Russian-language interpreter for presidents Reagan, Bush, and Clinton at all super-power summits.

When we turn to the Rusyn-American involvement in European affairs, the picture is quite different. As early as 1904, the Greek Catholic Union's president Michael Yuhasz, Sr. and its editor Pavel Zatkovich participated with Slovaks in a congress which sent a memorandum to the Hungarian government protesting the treatment of their brethren in the homeland. For their part, both Hungary and Russia were greatly interested in immigrant activity, especially before World War I. We have already seen how Russia's tsarist government liberally supported the Orthodox movement, while Budapest, through local Austro-Hungarian consulates in Pittsburgh, New York City, and Cleveland as well as through its Trans-Atlantic Trust Company in New York City, tried to keep Carpatho-Rusyns loyal to Hungary and separated from fellow Slavs, especially Slovaks and Galician Rusyns of the Russophile or Ukrainophile orientation.

82. Homestead Resolution as it appeared on the pages of the *Amerikansky russky viestnik*, August 8, 1918.

It was toward the end of World War I that the Rusyn-American community was to have its greatest impact on the fate of the homeland. Among the first to organize were the Orthodox Lemkos from Galicia, who under the leadership of a newly arrived political leader Peter P. Hatalak established in early 1917 the League for the Liberation of Carpatho-Russia (Sojuz Osvoboždenija Prikarpatskoj Rusi). The League published the newspaper *Prikarpatskaja Rus'* (New York, 1917-25) and began to collect funds to aid the war-torn homeland. To publicize its cause further, the League organized in New York City on July 13, 1917 the first Carpatho-Russian Congress (Karpatorusskij Kongress) in America. Its goal was to work for the "unification of all Carpatho-Russian lands"—that is, Galicia, Bukovina, and Hungarian or Subcarpathian Rus'—with a democratic Russia. Most of the supporters of the congress were Lemkos and other Russophiles from Galicia; and while the Orthodox Church was well represented, no Subcarpathian Byzantine Catholic priests were present, since they still felt that their loyalties lay with Hungary.

Even more important was the arrival in the United States of Professor Tomáš G. Masaryk, the

81. Czechoslovak President Tomáš G. Masaryk.

83. Gregory I. Zatkovich as governor of Subcarpathian Rus', authographed and dated 1920.

Slavic leader who was working on behalf of the creation of an independent state of Czechoslovakia. While consulting with Czech and Slovak immigrant leaders in Pittsburgh in May 1918, Masaryk also met with Nicholas Pachuta, the head of an organization called the American Russian National Defense (Amerikansko-Russka Narodna Obrana). This group had been founded in 1915 in Braddock, Pennsylvania and drew most of its supporters from the recent converts to Orthodoxy led by Bishop Stephen (Alexander) Dzubay. Although Pachuta originally supported the idea of union with Russia, he now urged that his countrymen in America favor instead the idea of joining the Czechs and Slovaks in their proposed new state.

What was to prove more significant, however, was the meeting on July 23, 1918 of Byzantine Ruthenian Catholic clerical and lay leaders from the Greek Catholic Union and United Societies. Meeting in Homestead, Pennsylvania (a suburb of Pittsburgh), they formed the American Council of Uhro-Rusins (Amerikanska Narodna Rada Uhro-Rusinov). Headed by Father Nicholas Chopey and Julius Gardoš, this council proclaimed itself the only legal representative of Carpatho-Rusyns in the

United States and proposed three possible political alternatives for the homeland after the end of World War I: (1) autonomy within Hungary; (2) unity with fellow Rusyns in neighboring Galicia and Bukovina; or (3) autonomy within an unspecified state.

Convinced that as a member of the Entente the United States would play a decisive role in the postwar redrawing of Europe's boundaries, and in order to be confident of success while operating in an otherwise alien American political environment, the American Council of Uhro-Rusins engaged Gregory I. Zatkovich to seek the best political alternative for the homeland. Although born in Subcarpathian Rus', Zatkovich had been educated from grade school in the United States and was working at the time as a lawyer for General Motors. Moreover, he was thoroughly versed in Carpatho-Rusyn community affairs since his recently deceased father, Pavel, had been the founding editor of the Greek Catholic Union's *Amerikansky russky viestnik,* and his brother, Theophile, was a priest and later chancellor of the Byzantine Ruthenian Catholic eparchy in Pittsburgh. Along with his important connections, the then 32-year-old Gregory Zatkovich was an extremely dynamic individual and clearly the best political lobbyist available to Carpatho-Rusyn Americans.

By October, Zatkovich had met with President Woodrow Wilson and other American officials, and he had registered the Uhro- (Subcarpathian) Rusyns as a separate people in the Mid-European Union organized in Philadelphia under the

84. United States President Woodrow Wilson.

leadership of Masaryk. Zatkovich then convinced the Carpatho-Rusyn immigrants it would be best if Rusyns were to join the newly established republic of Czechoslovakia. In order to legitimize the Czechoslovak orientation, a vote was taken throughout the lodges of the largest Greek Catholic fraternal societies, the Greek Catholic Union and United Societies. The result was 68 percent of the lodges in favor of union with Czechoslovakia. Satisfied with this result, Zatkovich led a Rusyn-American delegation in early 1919 to the Paris Peace Conference and to the homeland where local leaders, overjoyed with the decision of their brethren in America, formed a congress at Užhorod on May 8, 1919. The Užhorod council accepted the

Rusyn-American proposal and called for the incorporation into Czechoslovakia of all Rusyn-inhabited territory south of the Carpathians. In September, the peacemakers in Paris approved the Czechoslovak solution to the Rusyn problem. Recognizing the role of Rusyn Americans in postwar international politics, in 1919, Czechoslovakia's founding president Tomáš Masaryk appointed Zatkovich—though he was still an American citizen—as president of the Directorium and then, in 1920, as first governor of Subcarpathian Rus' (Czech: *Podkarpatská Rus).*

But Zatkovich's European political career did not last long. In 1921, he resigned in protest after Czechoslovakia refused to grant autonomy and to

85. Members of the Mid-European Union before a replica of America's Liberty Bell in Independence Hall, Philadelphia, October 1918. In the center (with glasses and white beard) is the union's chairman, Professor Tomáš G. Masaryk; standing in the back to the left of the bell is the Rusyn representative, Gregory Zatkovich. The bell was sent the following year as a memorial to Užhorod, the capital of Subcarpathian Rus'.

86. The Central Rusyn National Council in Užhorod greets the Rusyn-American delegation and proclaims its unity with Czechoslovakia, May 8, 1919. Alongside Gregory Zatkovich (behind the folk-costumed woman) is his successor as governor, Antonij Beskyd (on the right) and the future premier-minister of the Carpatho-Ukraine, Monsignor Avhustyn Vološyn (on the left).

87. The American Rusin National Congress, Homestead, Pennsylvania, September 15-16, 1919, greets Gregory Zatkovich before his return to the European homeland. Father Nicholas Chopey, chairman of the congress, is the third person seated to the right of the youthful Zatkovich (front row center). Photo by Fischer and Haller.

88. Third Carpatho-Russian Congress, New York City, December 28-31, 1919. Seated in the second row center are the Russophile politicians from Galicia, Dr. Dmitry Markov (on the left) and Dmitry Vergun (on the right).

unite the approximately 100,000 Carpatho-Rusyns—living "temporarily" in eastern Slovakia—with the province of Subcarpathian Rus'. After returning to Pittsburgh, Zatkovich published various pamphlets criticizing Czechoslovakia, and he was soon joined by GCU president Michael Yuhasz, Sr., who organized the Rusin Council for National Defense at Pittsburgh on November 28, 1922. In the name of this council, Yuhasz sent several protests to the League of Nations in Geneva and to the Czechoslovak government in Prague. The original complaints concerned the administrative division and lack of autonomy for the Carpatho-Rusyn homeland. Now, too, there were accusations that the Prague government was allowing Ukrainians from Galicia to dominate the cultural affairs of the province.

Since Zatkovich's experiences abroad had been well publicized, no Rusyn-American newspaper or organization during the 1920s and 1930s was willing to recognize the many economic, social, and cultural achievements brought about by the Prague government in the homeland. Instead, Rusyn-American publicists continued to harp on the supposed "injustices" of Czechoslovak rule. Furthermore, some Subcarpathian politicians (Antonij Beskyd, Stefan Fencyk) travelled to the United States where they assured themselves of financial backing for their anti-Czechoslovak ventures.

By the 1930s, while Byzantine Catholic Carpatho-Rusyns were deeply involved in the celi-

bacy issue, the initiative for political activity was taken up by Orthodox leaders. They kept up the attack on Czechoslovakia through a new organization, the Carpatho-Russian Union (Karpatorusskij Sojuz), established in Pittsburgh in June 1933. This group was under the leadership of Dr. Aleksej Gerovsky, a staunch Orthodox spokesman and recently arrived émigré, who had been forced to leave Czechoslovakia because of his anti-government and Russophile proselytizing activities among the Carpatho-Rusyns. In an attempt to rise above the religious controversies, the Carpatho-Russian Union included Orthodox Rusyns as well as several leaders from the Greek Catholic Union. The dynamic Gerovsky also set up his own press agency in New York City under the name KARUS. Gerovsky's anti-Czechoslovak sentiment was so great that it was not long before his demands for Rusyn autonomy led to a call for border revisionism, thereby resulting in cooperation with Hungarian governmental representatives in the United States and western Europe as well as with pro-Hungarian Rusyn politicians from the homeland.

Among the latter was Stefan Fencyk, a Rusyn parliamentary representative who was hosted by Gerovsky in 1935 on a grand tour of Rusyn-American communities, to raise funds for further anti-Czechoslovak political activity in the homeland. Gerovsky's influence reached its highest point in the summer of 1938, when he led a delegation of the Carpatho-Russian Union that held talks with the Czechoslovak government in Prague and then went eastward to Subcarpathian Rus' to foster, with some success, the formation of a political coalition between local Russophiles and Ukrainophiles who were working to achieve autonomy.

Considering the general Russophile and Rusynophile national orientations that prevailed during the 1930s among the majority of Rusyn-American spokespersons and their organizations, it is not surprising that most of the community expressed opposition to the "Ukrainian regime" headed by the Greek Catholic priest, Avhustyn Vološyn, and Minister Julian Revay, which came to power in Subcarpathian Rus' and renamed the region Carpatho-Ukraine during its few months of autonomy between October 1938 and March 1939. The only exception to the general anti-Ukrainian trend was the Committee for the Defense of Carpatho-Ukraine (Komitet Oborony Karpats'koji Ukrajiny), a small group headed by Father Emil Nevicky, which tried to convince Rusyn Americans to support Vološyn's Carpatho-Ukrainian government. But the Carpatho-Russian Union as well as the GCU and other Byzantine Catholic organizations were so angered by what they considered the Ukrainian "encroachment" that they did not even speak out against the forcible return of Hungarian rule in their homeland after March 1939.

In fact, the first group to protest the political changes in Europe was the Lemko Association, which under the leadership of Petro Guzlej, Michael Mahonec, Dmitry Vislocky, and Dr. Simeon Pysh, set up a Carpatho-Russian National Committee in New York City on February 11, 1939. In subsequent months, this committee called for the unification of all Carpatho-Rusyn lands—whether in Poland, Slovakia, or Hungary—with the Soviet Union. However, following the outbreak of World War II in September 1939, the pro-Soviet position of the Lemko Association and its National Committee became suspect in the eyes of American authorities, because at that time the Soviet Union was allied with Nazi Germany. Then came Germany's invasion of the Soviet Union in June 1941, after which Stalin's "Communist Russians" became allies of the United States. It was now acceptable for Americans to praise Soviet Russia and still be patriotic.

Capitalizing on this new situation, the Lemko Carpatho-Russian National Committee joined with the Carpatho-Russian Union (which by then had

lost the support of the Byzantine Catholics and the Greek Catholic Union) to form, in July 1942, a new American Carpatho-Russian Congress (Amerikanskyj Karpatorusskij Kongress) headed by Peter Ratica. It was through this organization that Rusyn Americans (mostly Russophile-oriented Lemkos and Orthodox) contributed to the Russian War Relief, raising close to $100,000 for food, clothing, and other supplies destined for the Red Army. It is interesting to note, however, that the American Carpatho-Russian Congress did not call for the future incorporation of the homeland with the Soviet Union, but only for the unity of all Carpatho-Rusyn territory (the Lemko Region, Prešov Region, and Subcarpathian Rus') and for its autonomy to be guaranteed in some unspecified state.

Meanwhile, it was not until three years into the war that the vast majority of Carpatho-Rusyns in America (that is, those from the Prešov Region and Subcarpathian Rus') finally took a clear stand on the fate of their homeland south of the Carpathians. Following the disintegration of Czechoslovakia in March 1939, Subcarpathian Rus' was ruled by Hungary and the Prešov Region by the pro-German independent state of Slovakia. Gregory

89. Leaders of the American Carpatho-Russian Central Conference meet with officials of the Czechoslovak government-in-exile, May 23, 1943. Seated from left to right: Gregory Zatkovich, President Eduard Beneš, Dr. Paul Cibere, and John Primich. The clergyman standing (second from the left) is Father Ivan Ladižinsky.

Zatkovich, head of the Byzantine Catholic American Carpatho-Russian Council of Pittsburgh, and Father Ivan A. Ladižinsky, head of the Orthodox Carpatho-Russian Unity of Gary, Indiana, dropped their differences and on March 22, 1942 united into one American Carpatho-Russian Central Conference. Based in Pittsburgh, this new organization reversed the direction of two decades of criticism directed against Czechoslovakia and instead agreed to work with that government's representatives in exile (led by former President Eduard Beneš and Minister Jan Masaryk) to restore Subcarpathian Rus' after World War II as an equal partner in a renewed Czechoslovak state. Such a policy also coincided with the war aims of the United States and its other allies, including the Soviet Union.

Hence, the Carpatho-Rusyns were very surprised to find at the end of the war that Subcarpathian Rus' did not become part of a restored Czechoslovakia, but rather was incorporated into the Soviet Union in June 1945. They were especially shocked to learn that the Soviet government had initiated a policy of Ukrainianization and that it had begun to undermine and before long to liquidate the Greek (or Byzantine-rite) Catholic Church. Protests to the United States State Department and to the newly founded United Nations Organization in San Francisco were sent in 1945, and the following year in August a special Carpatho-Russian Congress was convened in Munhall, Pennsylvania to protest Soviet rule in the homeland. But these acts proved to be of no avail. The most the immigrants could do was to deny money, food, clothing, and other supplies from the Carpatho-Russian Relief Fund to Soviet-held territory and to supply these only to Carpatho-Rusyns in northeastern Slovakia, which had not yet come under Soviet-inspired Communist rule.

In 1951, a Council of a Free Sub-Carpatho-Ruthenia in Exile (Rada Svobodnoj Podkarpatskoj Rusi v Exili) was founded in Hamilton, Ontario by Vasilij V. Fedinec, the former president of the Subcarpathian Bank in Užhorod and recent immigrant to Canada. This council worked closely with the Byzantine Ruthenian Catholic Church in the United States, and through its organ, *Rusin/Ruthenian* (New York and Hamilton, Ont., 1952-60), joined with other Czechoslovak émigré groups in protesting the Soviet annexation of Subcarpathian Rus' in 1945 and the imposition of Communist

rule in Czechoslovakia in 1948. The Greek Catholic Union also continued to urge American authorities to help free their brethren in Subcarpathian Rus' *(Pod-Karpatskaja Rus')*, and at its 1964 convention it even adopted a resolution calling on the United Nations to act, "so that Carpatho-Russia be recognized and accepted into the free nations of the world as an autonomous state."[11] But none of these efforts were to have any impact. Clearly, the decisive political influence that Carpatho-Rusyn immigrants had once been able to exert over events in Europe following World War I was no longer possible in the post-1945 world.

The last organized attempt at political action was undertaken by the Lemko Relief Committee in the United States, founded in June 1946 by industrialist Peter S. Hardy and the Orthodox priest, Joseph Simko of Trumbull, Connecticut. Several thousand dollars were collected to aid Lemkos who, after their forced deportation in 1947 to various parts of Communist-ruled Poland, wanted to return to their Carpathian villages. After 1957, the Polish government allowed Hardy to visit the area and to distribute some funds which were used mainly to purchase food and clothing and to reconstruct damaged churches. The following year, through Hardy's personal intervention, the Polish government signed a fifteen-point document agreeing to continue the aid program. This unprecedented act for a Communist government—undertaken, moreover, at the height of the Cold War—was probably related to the fact that Hardy was a long-time supporter of the pro-Soviet Lemko Association in Yonkers, New York. Whatever the reason, the aid program had limited practical results, since the vast majority of Lemkos have until this day been unable to return from other parts of Poland to their ancestral Carpathian homeland.

The aid program carried out by the Lemko Relief Committee after World War II points to another important aspect of Rusyn-American relations with the European homeland—the economic impact. Before World War I, but especially

---

[11] Cited in John Masich, "Highlights in the Glorious History of the Greek Catholic Union of the U.S.A.," in *Jubilee Almanac of the Greek Catholic Union of the U.S.A.*, LXXI, ed. Michael Roman (Munhall, Pa., 1967), p. 263.

between 1919 and 1938, immigrant workers sent thousands of dollars in cash and goods to their families in Europe. This spontaneous, familial-based channelling of funds did in fact make a real difference. It helped numerous Rusyn families survive economic hardship, especially that brought on by the world depression of the 1930s.

More organized economic aid came in the form of bonds and other fund-raising activities carried out by Rusyn-American organizations. At least two financial institutions that operated at various times during the interwar years—the Subcarpathian Bank in Užhorod, the administrative center of Subcarpathian Rus', and the Russian Bank in Mukačevo, the region's second largest city—were established, in part, with Rusyn-American investments.

Although immediately after World War II, Rusyn Americans could no longer send aid to Soviet-held Subcarpathian Rus' or to the Lemko Region

in Poland (which was being forcibly depopulated), they were able at least for a few years to send or purchase food, medicine, and clothing which was distributed mainly by the United Nations Relief and Recovery Administration (UNRRA) to Carpatho-Rusyns living in the Prešov Region of Czechoslovakia. Even though after 1948, the Cold War interrupted these contacts with Communist Czechoslovakia, by the 1960s the flow of money and goods on an individual basis was renewed. This has been supplemented further by United States social security and worker's compensation payments to the widows of the early immigrants. As a result, at least one region, eastern Slovakia, had in the last two decades of Communist rule (before 1989) acquired a reputation for affluence. It was not uncommon, for instance, to find elderly Rusyns in the Prešov Region with substantial bank accounts, or to hear tales of the "legendary *babas*"

90. A bond from the Subcarpathian Bank in Užhorod, designed by the noted Carpatho-Rusyn painter, Josyf Bokšaj, and made out to a Rusyn-American in the 1920s.

91. The Russian Bank in Mukačevo, Subcarpathian Rus',
founded in 1930 primarily with Rusyn-American funding.

(grandmothers) who purchase new automobiles for
their children and grandchildren with cash acquired
"from America" as a result of the benefits (social
security, worker's compensation) coming to them
from the former employment of their long-
deceased husbands.

Rusyn political involvement in Europe was
essentially a first-generation phenomenon. After
World War II, the vast majority of the older immi-
grants and their descendants became basically
apolitical and had virtually no concern with the
fate of the homeland when it was part of
Communist-ruled Czechoslovakia and the Soviet
Union. Only among the Lemko immigrants from
Polish Galicia (especially those who arrived after
World War II) was there some political activism as
expressed through publications and manifestations
led at times by the Lemko Association, the Lemko
Relief Committee, and most especially by the
Organization for the Defense of the Lemko Land.

Apart from an interest in the fate of the European homeland, for most Carpatho-Rusyn immigrants and their descendants even before World
War II, politics has usually meant and still means
the debates and controversies that surround national identity. This problem is, of course, intimately
related to relations with other ethnic groups, especially Ukrainians and Slovaks, and to a lesser
degree, Russians and Hungarians.

Although it was quite understandable for the
earliest newcomers to tell immigration officials
that they were from Austria, or Hungary, or Poland, or Czechoslovakia, they at the same time
knew very well that ethnically, linguistically, and

culturally they were neither Austrian, nor Hungarian, nor Polish, nor Czech, nor Slovak. Their
Rusyn dialectal speech and/or their Greek Catholic
or Orthodox faith clearly set them off from the
other groups. Thus, a Rusyn identity was the most
common denominator among the pre-World War
I immigrants.

Nonetheless, frequent interaction with related
groups in the United States and the use from time
to time of English often prompted a discussion, or
at least self-reflection, on the question of national
or ethnic identity. (In the European homeland,
where one rarely left the native village, the question of national or ethnic identity hardly ever
arose.) Assuming that the term *Rusyn* (or *Rusin*)
was not acceptable usage in English, many community spokespersons and organizations began to
describe themselves as Russian or sometimes Carpatho-Russian, even if they knew, at least initially,
that they were different from the Russians of
Russia (whom they often designated as Musco-
vites).

It was not too long before some leaders,
especially from among the second generation,
began to use the name *Russian* not simply as a
self-perceived acceptable term in English, but as a
description of the group's ostensible ethnic
affiliation. To be sure, such Russophile views had
also been prevalent in the European homeland both
before and after World War I, that is, views that
the Carpatho-Rusyns were simply a branch of one
unified Russian people that inhabited an extensive
territory stretching from the Carpathian Mountains
to the Pacific Ocean. It was beliefs such as these
that led some Rusyn-American editors to attempt
to publish in Russian in the community's
newspapers, attempts which generally resulted in
a strange, uncodified, and often comical language.

For the most part, there have been at least
four trends or orientations prevalent among
Carpatho-Rusyn Americans regarding their nation-
al/ethnic identity: (1) that the group forms a
distinct East Slavic nationality known as Rusyn,
Rusnak, Ruthenian, Carpatho-Rusyn, or Uhro-
Rusin; (2) that the group is part of either the Russian nationality; (3) the Slovak nationality; or (4)
the Ukrainian nationality. It is interesting to note
that for some individuals it is possible to be simultaneously a Rusyn and a Russian, or a Rusyn
(Rusnak) and Slovak; or a Rusyn and Ukrainian.

Not surprisingly, in the United States, where there was never any official or legal need for the group to have a fixed identity, the situation has remained from the outset very fluid. With regard to the community's organizational structure, it might be said that at least through World War I, the largest religious and secular organizations—the Greek (Byzantine Ruthenian) Catholic Church and the Greek Catholic Union—accepted the view that the group formed a distinct nationality. By the late 1920s and 1930s, however, the Greek Catholic Union's leaders, especially Peter Zeedick and Michael Roman, referred to the group as Russian and adopted a Russophile view. The Byzantine Catholic Church, meanwhile, although it adopted the term *Ruthenian*, more and more associated that name with a specific religious body (which could and did include Slovaks, Hungarians, and Croats as well as Rusyns). The church preferred not to associate itself with any one ethnic group. Consequently, Ruthenian, and later by extrapolation Byzantine, became an identity, like Catholic or Jewish, and was perceived to be sufficient as an ethnic or national self-descriptor.

On the other hand, those Carpatho-Rusyns who joined Orthodox churches during the several waves of defections from Byzantine Catholicism, almost without exception adopted from the beginning the term *Russian* as an identifier, so that many so-called "Russians" or persons of "Russian descent" in the United States have no awareness that their roots really go back to Subcarpathian Rus' or the Lemko lands north of the Carpathians, and that the Slavic population there is neither ethnically nor linguistically Russian.

There are also smaller groups of post-World War II immigrants and their descendants who identify as Ukrainians; while others, who know their parents or grandparents are from territories that are now within Slovakia, consider themselves Slovaks. Finally, beginning in the 1970s, with the general interest in ethnicity and the search for roots in American society, there has been a revival of the original term *Rusyn*, sometimes spelled *Rusin*. It is being used more and more in secular and religious (especially Byzantine Catholic) publications in the form *Carpatho-Rusyn* or *Carpatho-Ruthenian*, and with the connotation that it describes a distinct ethnic group.

As might be expected, the changing self-perceptions and the use of so many terms to describe the same people has caused controversy not only among Carpatho-Rusyns themselves but also friction and misunderstandings with the other groups whose identity may have been adopted. The Russian community, for instance, has generally ignored the specific characteristics of Carpatho-Rusyn culture, even though it is the Rusyns, whether from Subcarpathia and especially the Lemko Region, who make up significant portions of Russian Orthodox parishes. The traditional Russian view, after all, is that the population in question is just a dialectal branch of the Russian nation.

Ignorance and even conflict have often marked relations between Carpatho-Rusyns on the one hand and Slovaks or Ukrainians on the other. Slovak-American publications in the past (and some still today) have argued that the term *Rusnak* simply means a Byzantine-rite Catholic from Slovakia. Following that line of thinking, all Carpatho-Rusyns/Rusnaks whose ancestors stem from present-day Slovakia must be considered Slovaks. Views like these have prompted certain Slovak-American publications to describe the Byzantine Ruthenian Catholic Church and the Greek Catholic Union as Slovak organizations.

Relations between Carpatho-Rusyns and Ukrainians in the United States have been strained even more. We have already seen in Chapter 4 how regional and ethnic conflicts between Subcarpathia and Galicia led, in 1916 and 1924, to the formal division of the Greek Catholic Church into Ruthenian and Ukrainian separate administrations, then eparchies, and subsequently metropolitanates. The two communities have continued to remain far apart. Ukrainians argue that *Rusyn* is just their own antiquated name, so that all Carpatho-Rusyns are simply Ukrainians, while Carpatho-Rusyns respond that Ukrainians are ethnically different and usually political extremists more concerned with nationalism than with religious concerns and Christian spirituality.

Arguments such as those summarized above have characterized public statements and private sentiments throughout the almost century-long interaction of Carpatho-Rusyns, Russians, Slovaks, and Ukrainians in the United States. On the other hand, it must be admitted that for most Carpatho-Rusyns, who today are of the second-, third-, and fourth-generation, arguments over national or ethnic identity are at best academic if not irrelevant. Since World War I, the vast majority of the group's members have preferred to consider themselves first and foremost Americans, perhaps of the Byzantine Catholic or Orthodox faith. And if they need to think about their ethnic identity, a vague association with the concept Rus' or perhaps more generally Slavic is more than sufficient for their heritage and associational needs.

Chapter 8

Group Maintenance

The problem of the lack of a consistent identity, discussed at the end of the previous chapter, has had a significant impact on the ability of Carpatho-Rusyns to sustain a sense of ethnic commitment and group maintenance in the United States. In fact, the majority of third- and fourth-generation descendants of the original immigrants have at best only a vague idea of their heritage and very little awareness of its relationship to a specific territorial entity called Carpathian Rus' or Carpatho-Ruthenia.

The reasons for this are many. First, because the vast majority of Carpatho-Rusyn immigrants came here before World War I, their grandchildren and great-grandchildren more than half a century later are fully acculturated, even assimilated, into mainstream American society. In this context, it was the second generation—the sons and daughters of the original immigrants born or raised primarily in the United States—who were often the most active assimilators. While they were familiar with the Old-World heritage and at least had a passive if not active knowledge of some Carpatho-Rusyn dialect, these "American assimilators" more often than not deliberately chose to forget the past and to make sure that they and their children were just the same as all other Americans.

In the process of loosening ties to the past, language was the first characteristic to be lost. The first-generation immigrants still spoke their native Rusyn dialects, but these became laden with Americanisms quite quickly. In any case, English was urged upon the children, and the speech of the old country was denigrated as simply "our language" *(po-našomu)*. It was not viewed as having any particular value in the "real" American world.

Even if the first or second generation did try to pass on some Old-World language to their children, more than likely they would tell them that they were speaking Russian (that is, "soft Russian" as opposed to "hard Russian") or "Slavish"/"Slavonic." The first interpretation was incorrect; the second meant nothing. Moreover, it is not surprising to find many younger descendants of Carpatho-Rusyns, who have gone to college in greater numbers recently, attending Russian-language courses in which they were puzzled by encounters with American-trained teachers who ironically would refer to the few dialectal words or pronunciations they may remember from their family as "kitchen Russian."

Furthermore, outside the home, the use of Carpatho-Rusyn is hardly to be encountered anywhere. Church services are entirely in English, although a few liturgies are still being said in Church Slavonic (a liturgical language far from spoken Carpatho-Rusyn). We have also seen that, with the exception of portions of the Lemko Association's newspaper *(Karpatska Rus')*, all other religious and fraternal publications are in English. Thus, when the now very old pre-World War I immigrants have passed on, spoken Carpatho-Rusyn in America will die as well. For Carpatho-Rusyns in the United States, as with many other similar groups, language maintenance is virtually non-existent.

Another difficulty for group maintenance is related to the larger American educational and social context. In effect, young people have had nothing concrete to relate to if they are ever exposed to the concept Carpathian Rus' or Carpatho-Ruthenia. Such names no longer appear on maps, and until very recently there were no adequate popular or scholarly books about the region written in English. In addition, it is extremely difficult, if not impossible, for Americans, even those with a higher education, to understand that ethnic or national identity is not necessarily coincident with the state in which one lives. Few are aware of the reality that not everyone who lives in France is French, or in Slovakia Slovak, or in the former Soviet Union Russian. To be sure, such misperceptions are not easy to change in an American social and educational context, which at the elementary, high school, and college level is woefully inadequate in terms of its coverage or exposure to east-central Europe.

Even the renewed contact with the homeland, which began slowly in the late 1960s, did not at first help very much. The reasons had to do with political policies and societal evolution. When the Soviet Union annexed Subcarpathian Rus' (Transcarpathia) to the Ukrainian S.S.R. in 1945, the Communist authorities declared by fiat that the nationality problem was resolved. All Rusyns, regardless what they may have called themselves, were officially declared to be Ukrainian. This approach was adopted as well by the Soviet-influenced governments of Poland and (after 1948) Czechoslovakia. Therefore, officially—and for the most part in practice as well—Rusyns ceased to exist in the Carpathian homeland.

Consequently, when immigrants and their descendants did begin to visit the Europe they had once left or had heard about from parents, they were often struck by the fact that they could not understand the language of the people they met. In Soviet Transcarpathia, standard Ukrainian was generally spoken, while in the administrative center of Užhorod—where visitors were expected to stay and to meet their relatives from the villages—Russian was in most cases the language of formal and official communication. As for the Lemko Region north of the Carpathians in Poland, the indigenous Lemko Rusyns were voluntarily or forcibly evacuated in 1946-1947, and their places were taken by Poles. Finally, in the Prešov Region of northeastern Slovakia, to which most American tourists flocked, the old people may have still spoken Rusyn dialects, but the younger generations used Slovak exclusively, most likely did not attend an Eastern-rite or any church, and more often than not were anxious to reject their Rusyn/Rusnak/East Slavic heritage in favor of a Slovak identity.

Thus, in a situation where the spoken Carpatho-Rusyn dialects in the United States were not being maintained, where the American educational system provided no suitable information, and where even travel to the homeland did not contribute to an understanding of the traditional culture, it was not surprising that second-, third-, and fourth-generation descendants of Carpatho-Rusyn immigrants, if they were conscious of their heritage at all, were likely to associate with groups that had some kind of contemporary political existence, whether Russian, or Slovak, sometimes even Ukrainian. Even more likely, however, if asked about ethnic or national identity, a Carpatho-Rusyn American would simply respond with a religious affiliation—Byzantine Catholic (often raised to the category of national identity) or Orthodox.

For their part, the churches and their leaders always felt uneasy about the ethnic or national factor. On the one hand, it was ethnic or territorial specificity which made possible the existence of individual religious bodies. Otherwise, why should not all Byzantine-rite Catholics (Ruthenians, Ukrainians, Arabic Melkites) or all Orthodox (Carpatho-Russians, Belorusans, Greeks, Russians, and so forth) be united in a single Catholic or single Orthodox jurisdiction. It was ethnic and/or territorial distinctions, therefore, which often provided the justification, at least initially, for individual religious bodies, each of which today has its own bishops and jealously guarded hierarchical structures.

On the other hand, those same ethnic distinctions and, as we have seen, debates about identity often caused discord that frequently led to disunity, defections, and rivalry within and between churches. Therefore, church hierarchs frequently discussed religion and ethnicity or nationalism as mutually exclusive phenomena. In simplest terms, religion and politics did not mix. It is not surprising, therefore, that the Byzantine Ruthenian hierarchs have at least since World War II spoken of all their parishioners (regardless of their ethnic origins) simply as Byzantine Catholics—the official name of the church, *Ruthenian*, being understood as referring to rite, not nationality. Similarly, we have seen how historically the Russian Orthodox Church in the United States (both the Metropolia and Patriarchal Exarchate) repeatedly thwarted all attempts to set up a viable "Carpatho-Russian" diocese. And with the establishment of the Orthodox Church in America in 1970, the term Russian was dropped entirely from its name with the church following an official policy that de-emphasized ethnic differences in what was to be considered simply an American religious body of Orthodox Christian persuasion. In this regard, only the small "Johnstown" Orthodox diocese has been consistent in fostering a sense of "Carpatho-Russian" ethnic and cultural distinctiveness among its members.

Nonetheless, despite all the negative aspects regarding group maintenance and ethnic identity, it still must be said that many Carpatho-Rusyns continue to cling in some way to their traditional heritage. It is true that the traditional mechanisms that have maintained ethnic awareness in the past —Rusyn language use in families, in churches, and in newspapers; ethnic schools; dramatic clubs—no longer exist. Nonetheless, both the churches and fraternal societies still provide settings in which old familial and friendship associational patterns are retained. Individual parishes bring together people for religious services, weddings, and other social functions such as dances, bingo nights, and "pirohy-making nights," the extensive income from which validates the often unrecognized fact that it is the women who have built and supported the churches. And despite the generally cautious attitude of the church toward ethnicity, it is still at the individual parish level, whether in the Byzantine Ruthenian Catholic Church, Orthodox Church in America, or "Johnstown" Orthodox diocese, where the new folk ensembles, with participation among children and parents, have been founded. Similarly, the fraternal societies, especially the widespread Greek Catholic Union, have through individual lodges continued to provide bowling and golf clubs and summer resorts where community ties are continually reinforced. Hence, in sociological

terms, Carpatho-Rusyns in America still form a group or groups, whose members are united by common kinship, religion, and social ties, regardless of what they might call themselves.

There are, moreover, other factors which in the past two decades have contributed to raising the level of consciousness among Americans of Rusyn background. These factors are related to developments in the United States as well as in the European homeland. Since the 1970s, new cultural organizations like the Carpatho-Rusyn Research Center have flourished. For instance, during its first sixteen years of existence, that center distributed by 1993 over 24,000 publications and published 64 issues of a quarterly magazine, all of which have dealt specifically with the Carpatho-Rusyn past and present.

The larger American society has discovered Carpatho-Rusyns as well. They figure as a distinct group with their own entry or volume in widely

92. Cover of a popular book on Carpatho-Rusyns in America, published in 1989, with an introduction by United States Senator Daniel Patrick Moynihan.

distributed publications such as the *Harvard Encyclopedia of American Ethnic Groups* (1980), the Chelsea House *Peoples of North America Series* (1989), the *Dictionary of American Immigration History* (1990), the volumes on America and Europe in Yale University's *Encyclopedia of World Cultures* (1992-94), and in the *Encyclopedia of New York City* (1993). Finally, the United States Census Bureau, after refining its ancestry categories, listed "Carpatho-Rusyn" as a distinct group in its 1990 census reports. In short, Rusyn Americans have been recognized for the first time by the host society of which they are a part.

Political developments in Europe, especially since the appearance in 1985 of Mikhail Gorbachev in the former Soviet Union and the revolutions of 1989 throughout east-central Europe, have also had a profound impact on Rusyn-American life. In a real sense, during the century-long Carpatho-Rusyn presence in the United States, the degree of intensity of Rusyn self-awareness has been directly related to contacts with the homeland. When those contacts were strong, so was Carpatho-Rusyn group maintenance in the United States; when they were weak, a distinct Rusyn identity waned.

For a full half century that encompassed World War II and over four decades of Communist rule, Rusyn Americans were largely cut off from their relatives and friends in the European homeland. Even when travel was allowed, it was fraught with visa formalities and other restrictions that were characteristic of all Soviet-dominated police states. Then came Gorbachev and the Revolutions of 1989. The proverbial iron curtain was lifted, familial contacts that had been broken off so many years before were restored, and new relationships were forged. The fear of travelling to Communist countries ended, visa requirements were simplified or entirely abolished, and for the first time visitors could travel wherever they wished in Ukraine's Transcarpathian region. Moreover, with the fall of Communism and the very disintegration of the Soviet Union in late 1991, the Rusyn nationality question became once again a real issue.

With the end of censorship and the introduction of freedom of speech in the Soviet Ukraine, Czechoslovakia, and Poland, local Rusyns felt that for the first time in forty years they could

93. Archbishop Thomas V. Dolinay of Pittsburgh meets for the first time in the European homeland with Bishop Ivan Semedij of the Eparchy of Mukačevo, February 1990.

proclaim openly that they were Rusyns and not Ukrainians. In 1990, six new Rusyn organizations were founded in each country where Rusyns live (including Hungary, but excluding Romania), and Rusyn-language newspapers and magazines began to appear. The post-Communist Czechoslovak government even officially recognized Rusyns as a distinct nationality and recorded their numbers in its 1991 census. Finally, the Greek Catholic Church, which for decades had been the bulwark of a Rusyn national identity, was legalized in Ukraine and Poland and fully reconstituted in Slovakia (where it was restored in 1968).

In the course of these developments, Rusyns in each country where they live sought out and subsequently received encouragement and support from Carpatho-Rusyn religious and secular organizations in the United States. The Orthodox "Johnstown diocese" began already in 1989 to report on the plight of the Orthodox Church in eastern Slovakia. For its part, the Byzantine Ruthenian Catholic Church, led by Archbishops

Kocisko and Dolinay and Bishop Dudick, played a particularly active role in the reconstitution of the Greek Catholic Church. The entire American hierarchy travelled to Slovakia to be present at the formal installation of the new Greek Catholic bishop in Prešov in early 1990. Soon after that they reestablished relations with the Eparchy of Mukačevo in Ukraine, which has included the donation of funds raised in a campaign among American Rusyns to construct a Greek Catholic seminary in Užhorod. In response to the political changes and new realities in the European homeland, the Byzantine Ruthenian Seminary in Pittsburgh has since 1991 under the direction of Monsignor Russell A. Duker offered scholarships to seminarians from Transcarpathia and the Prešov Region and has made the study of Rusyn language and Rusyn history required subjects in its own curriculum.

As for secular organizations, among the first to become active in assisting the Carpatho-Rusyn homeland was the Andy Warhol Foundation in New York City. Inspired by its vice-president John Warhola, who was concerned about his family's Rusyn heritage, the foundation donated several paintings by Andy Warhol to a new Museum of Modern Art in the town of Medzilaborce, Slovakia, not far from the Carpatho-Rusyn village where both Warhol's parents were born. The Warhol Foundation also agreed to provide funds for an art school in Medzilaborce. The several gala functions held for the opening of the new museum that took place in 1991 in the presence of the Warhola family and Slovak government officials, all stressed the Rusyn aspect of the artist's ancestral heritage. Another New York City-based organization, the prestigious Institute for East-West Studies [IEWS], has also helped to get Rusyn Americans involved further in the democratization process in the European homeland of their ancestors. In early 1993, the IEWS, with financial support from a peace foundation in Japan and with the contractual agreement of the governments of post-Communist Poland, Slovakia, Ukraine, and Hungary, initiated through its Atlanta, Georgia office for regional development a Euro-Carpathian Region Project. Hailed as a model for regional cooperation in Europe, the goal of the Euro-Carpathian Project is to increase economic, human, and cultural ties between areas in four countries which virtually coincide with territory inhabited by Carpatho-Rusyns.

The Carpatho-Rusyn Research Center has, in particular, been involved in the homeland's recent national revival. The center represented Rusyn Americans at the First and Second World Congresses of Rusyns held in Medzilaborce, Slovakia (March 1991) and Krynica, Poland (May

94. Warhola Family Museum of Modern Art, Medzilaborce, Slovakia.

95. Members of the executive from the Ukraine, Slovakia, Poland, Yugoslavia, and the United States at the First World Congress of Rusyns, held in Medzilaborce, Slovakia, March 1991 (photo by Alexander Zozul'ák).

1993). In early 1992, it co-sponsored scholarly seminars at local universities in Užhorod (Ukraine), Cracow (Poland), Prešov (Slovakia), and Novi Sad (Yugoslavia); it cooperated in publishing books about Rusyns for readers in the homeland; and in November 1992 it co-sponsored with the Rusyn Renaissance Society (Rusyns'ka Obroda) in eastern Slovakia the First Congress of the Rusyn Language, whose goal is to codify a standard literary language for the group. Finally, in the wake of the war in Yugoslavia that, beginning in 1991, destroyed several Rusyn communities in eastern Croatia and then divided the rest of Vojvodinian Rusyns into two countries, the Carpatho-Rusyn Research Center initiated a Yugoslav Rusyn Youth fund to which American Rusyns have generously donated. The goal is to assist the Ruska Matka organization in Ruski Kerestur (Vojvodina) to prepare new school textbooks and to provide scholarships for local Rusyn students to study abroad. At the more popular level, the Slavjane Folk Ensemble from western Pennsylvania, sponsored by the Greek Catholic Union, participated en masse at the annual Rusyn folk festival in Medzilaborce in the summer of 1992.

Aside from the benefit such "American" contacts have for the homeland, they are particularly important for group maintenance in the United States. Today, Americans of Carpatho-Rusyn background, whether churchmen, scholars, cultural activists, or ordinary visitors, are able to travel easily to the ancestral homeland where they can

see real places and real people who speak Rusyn and who are proud of their Rusyn heritage. As a result, Rusyn Americans now come back home with a sense that their ethnic heritage is not some vague fairy-tale-like corpus of nostalgic reminiscences handed down by loving if somewhat mythologized grandparents, but rather that it is associated with a concrete place inhabited by real people of all ages and from all walks of life. Thus, the political changes in east-central Europe since 1989 have had, and are likely to continue to have, a positive impact on instilling in Rusyn Americans knowledge of and pride in their ancestral heritage.

Of course, it could also be argued that assimilation, or perhaps more appropriately adaptation to American society is a healthy thing. Unlike some other related ethnic groups, whose members are frequently uncertain of just where they belong, second-, third-, fourth-, and fifth-generation descendants of Carpatho-Rusyn immigrants function most comfortably as Americans. As Americans, all of whose forefathers came at one time or another from another continent, some Carpatho-Rusyns may even have an interest in their particular heritage. After all, it was American society itself which, during the Bicentennial Year and the decade of the 1970s, gave its official imprimatur to the roots fever that captured the imagination of much of the country.

In this context, Americans of Carpatho-Rusyn background continue to look to their past not as a substitute for what they already are—Americans—

but as another way to enrich their lives. It is such a spirit that has led some observers to speak of a recent "Rusyn renaissance" in America. How else can one explain the rise of more than a dozen folk groups, a marked increase in publications about the group, the success of cultural organizations such as the Carpatho-Rusyn Research Center, and the renewal of organizational and individual relations with the European homeland. Moreover, for the first time, all these activities are being carried out in a way in which the idea of a distinct Carpatho-Rusyn identity is accepted, even taken for granted. All things considered, it seems remarkable that several tens of thousands of poor, often illiterate immigrants arriving in America before World War I have produced offspring who several generations later, and several thousand miles from the European homeland, still in some way retain a sense of Carpatho-Rusyn identity.

96. Slavjane Folk Ensemble of McKees Rocks, Pennsylvania takes part in the parade prior to the Rusyn Folk Festival of Sport and Culture, in Medzilaborce, Slovakia, July 1992.

Chapter 9

Carpatho-Rusyns in Canada

As in the case of the United States, it is impossible to determine the exact number of Carpatho-Rusyns who immigrated to Canada. Estimates suggest that in the course of the twentieth century between 15,000 and 20,000 chose Canada as a new home. Most came after 1924, when immigration restrictions in the United States made entry there very difficult. It seems that the majority came from the Lemko Region in southern Galicia (then part of Poland), the rest from the Prešov Region of northeastern Slovakia, and even a few from the Bačka and Srem in Yugoslavia.

Although land was still relatively cheap in Canada during the 1920s, the Carpatho-Rusyn immigrants gravitated to urban industrial centers. Some settled in Montreal, Quebec, and farther west in Fort William (now part of Thunder Bay), Ontario, and Winnipeg, Manitoba. But the vast majority went to the southern Ontario cities of Toronto, Hamilton, Brantford, and Windsor. By the 1990s, as many as three quarters of Canada's Carpatho-Rusyns and their descendants lived in Toronto, the largest urban complex in Canada. The vast majority have found employment in the industrial complex of southern Ontario, including its many factories and the steel plants of Hamilton.

As in the United States, Carpatho-Rusyns in Canada are divided along religious, national, and political lines. The Byzantine-rite or Greek Catholics have come primarily from the Prešov Region in eastern Slovakia, but because they were few in number they did not have their own Greek Catholic Church as in the United States. Rather, they came under the jurisdiction of the Ukrainian Catholic Church in Canada. But not wanting to assimilate with Ukrainians, they were able to maintain a few parishes which were exclusively or largely made up of Rusyns or Rusnaks, as they called themselves. For instance, the first of these Byzantine-rite Rusyn churches was established in 1921 in the southern Alberta farming town of Lethbridge by immigrants who came from three ethnolinguistic Rusyn villages (Slovinky, Poráč, and Závadka) located in the old county of Szepes (Spiš) in the Prešov Region.

While the Greek Catholic immigrants from eastern Slovakia who arrived before World War II were for the most part ethnically Rusyn, those who came subsequently, especially during and just after the liberalization period in Czechoslovakia in 1968, were Slovaks. Despite the presence of this Slovak element and some efforts to have Byzantine-rite religious services conducted in the Slovak language, the older Rusyn immigrants have been able to maintain the use of the traditional Church Slavonic. The only other language used in churches is English.

The leadership of the Byzantine-rite Rusyns has opted for a Slovak identity, so that adherents of that religion (whether they are ethnically Rusyn or Slovak) have, since World War II, come to be known as Slovak Byzantine-rite Catholics. In

Town/City	Former Hungarian county or Galician district	Present country	Number of Rusyns 1910/1921	Percentage of Rusyns in total population
Lesko [P] (Lisko [P, U])	Lesko	Poland	285	8
Levoča [Sv] (Lőcse [H])	Szepes	Slovakia	201	3
Mukačeve [U] (Mukačevo [Ru]; Munkács [H])	Bereg	Ukraine	1,394	8
**Onokivci [U] (Felső-domonya [H]; Onokovci [Ru])	Ung	Ukraine	684	37
Posada Jaśliska [P] (Posada Jasliska [Ru])	Sanok	Poland	888	27
Rakošyn [Ru, U] (Beregrákos/ Rákos [H])	Bereg	Ukraine	2726	38
Sanok [P] (Sjanik [U])	Sanok	Poland	291	3
Seredne [U] (Seredn'oje [Ru]; Szerednye [H])	Ung	Ukraine	1867	34
Šid [Ru, SC] (Sid [H])	Szerem	Croatia	878	17
Sighetul Marmaţiei [Ro] (Máramarossziget [H]; Syhit [U]; Syhot [Ru])	Máramaros	Romania	532	3
Solotvyna [U] (Akna-Szlatina [H]; Solotvynski Kopal'ni [Ru])	Máramaros	Ukraine	209	9
Stari Vrbas [SC] (Óverbász [H]; Verbas [Ru]), today part of Vrbas	Bács-Bodrog	Yugoslavia	571	12
Tjačiv [U] (Técső [H]; Tjačovo [Ru])	Máramaros	Ukraine	855	14
**Torysky [Sv, U] (Tárcafő [H]; Toriskŷ [Ru]; Toriszka [H])	Szepes	Slovakia	775	21
Užhorod [Ru, U] (Ungvár [H])	Ung	Ukraine	641	4
Velykyj Bereznyj [Ru, U] (Nagyberezna [H])	Ung	Ukraine	1,120	40
Vişeul de Sus [Ro] (Vyšovo [U]; Felsőviső [H])	Máramaros	Romania	318	3
Vynohradiv [U] (Nagyszőllős [H]; Sevljuš [Ru])	Ugocsa	Ukraine	1,266	16
Vyškove [U] (Visk [H]; Vŷškovo nad Tysoju [Ru])	Máramaros	Ukraine	831	17

NOTE TO THE USER

The letters in brackets refer to the languages in which villages have been named:

[H]	Hungarian	[Sc]	Serbo-Croatian
[P]	Polish	[Sv]	Slovak
[Ro]	Romanian	[U]	Ukrainian
[Ru]	Rusyn		

The names of the former counties and districts are given in their Hungarian and Polish forms. Their equivalents in Rusyn are:

Hungarian	*Rusyn*	*Polish*	*Rusyn*
Marmaroš	Máramaros	Gorlice	Gorlyckŷ
Šaryš	Sáros	Grybów	Hrŷbov
Spiš	Szepes	Jasło	Jaslo
Srem	Szerem	Krosno	Krosno
Ugoča	Ugocsa	Lisko	Lŷysko
Už	Ung	Nowy Sącz	Novŷj Sanč
Zemplyn	Zemplén	Nowy Targ	Novŷj Torh

SOURCES: Statistical data are based on *A magyar szent korona országainak 1910 évi népszámlálása,* Magyar statisztikai közlemények, új sorozat, Vol. XLII (Budapest, 1912) and *Skorowidz miejscowości Rzeczypospolitej Polskiej opracowany na podstawie . . . spisu ludności 1921 r.,* Vol. XII: *Województwo Krakowskie/ Śląsk Cieszyński,* and Vol. XIII: *Województwo Lwowskie* (Warsaw, 1924-25).

Place name changes and supplemental statistical data were drawn from: *A magyar korona országainak 1900 évi népszámlálása,* Magyar statisztikai közlemények, új sorozat, Vol. I (Budapest, 1902); Stepan Tomašivs'kyj, "Etnohrafična karta Uhors'koji Rusy," in V.I. Lamanskij, ed., *Stat'i po slavjanovedeniju,* Vol. III (St. Petersburg, 1910); *Statistický lexikon obcí v republice československé . . . na základě výsledků sčítání lidu z 15. února 1921,* Vol. III: *Slovensko,* and Vol. IV: *Podkarpatská Rus* (Prague, 1927-28); *Retrospektívny lexikon obcí československej socialistickej republiky 1850-1970,* Vol. II, pt. 2: *abecedný prehľad obcí a částí obcí v rokoch 1850-1970* (Prague, 1978); *Istorija mist i sil Ukrajins'koji RSR: Zakarpats'ka torija mist i sil Ukrajins'koji RSR: Zakarpats'ka oblast'* (Kiev,

1969); *Istorija gorodov i sel Ukrainskoj SSR: Zakarpatskaja oblast'* (Kiev, 1982); *Šematyzm Hrekokatolyts'koho duchoven'stva apostol'skoji administraciji Lemkovščyny 1936,* 2nd ed. (Stamford, Conn., 1970); *Spis miejscowości Polskiej Rzeczypospolitej ludowej* (Warsaw, 1967); *Karpaty: obszar konwencji turystycznej* (Warsaw, 1967); *Bieszczady: mapa turystyczna, 1:75,000* (Warsaw, 1890); *Beskid Niski i Pogórze: mapa turystyczna, 1:125,000* (Warsaw, 1979); Volodymyr Kubijovyč, *Etnični hrupy pivdennozachidn'oji Ukrajiny (Halyčyny) na 1.1.1939* (Wiesbaden, 1983).

The Rusyn names, according to their official forms implemented in Subcarpathian Rus' in 1927, were taken from the 1921 Czechoslovak census (published in 1928). The Rusyn names for villages in Slovakia are taken from: Vasyl' Latta, *Atlas ukrajins'kych hovoriv Schidnoji Slovaččyny* (Bratislava and Prešov, 1991), pp. 24-26; for those in the Lemko Region from: Janusz Rieger, "Toponomastyka Beskidu Niskiego i Bieszczadów Zachodnich," in *Łemkowie: kultura— sztuka— język* (Warsaw and Cracow, 1987), pp. 135-168.

Village	Former Hungarian county or Galician district	Present administrative subdivision	Present country
Abranka [H, Ru, U]	Bereg	Volovec'	Ukraine
Abroncsos, *see* Obručné			
Aklos, *see* Uklyn			
Akna-Szlatina, *see* Solotvyna, p. 113			
Alsóalmád, *see* Nižná Jablonka			
Alsóapsa, *see* Dibrova, p. 112			
Alsóbaskócz, *see* Baškovce			
Alsóbistra, *see* Nyžnij Bystryj			
Alsócsebény, *see* Nižné Čabiny			
Alsódomonya, *see* Domanynci			
Alsófenyves, *see* Nižná Jedl'ová			
Alsógereben, *see* Nyžnja Hrabivnycja			
Alsóhatárszeg, *see* Nyžnja Roztoka			
Alsóhidekpatak, *see* Nyžnij Studenyj			
Alsóhimes, *see* Nižná Pisaná			
Alsóhunkócz, *see* Choňkovce			
Alsójedlova, *see* Nižná Jedl'ová			
Alsókálinfalva, *see* Kalyny			
Alsókalocsa, *see* Koločava			
Alsókaraszló, *see* Zariččja			
Alsókomárnok, *see* Nižný Komárnik			
Alsóladács, *see* Nižná Vladiča			
Alsó-Ladiskóc, *see* Nižné Čabiny			
Alsómerse, *see* Nižný Mirošov			
Alsónémeti, *see* Nižné Nemecké			
Alsóodor, *see* Nižný Orlík			
Alsóorlich, *see* Nižný Orlík			
Alsópagony, *see* Nižná Polianka			
Alsópásztély, *see* Behendjats'ka Pastil'			
Alsópiszana, *see* Nižná Pisaná			
Alsópolyánka, *see* Nižná Polianka			
Alsóremete, *see* Nyžni Remety			
Alsósárad, *see* Nyžnje Bolotne			
Alsószalánk, *see* Nižnie Slovinky			
Alsószelistye, *see* Nyžnje Selyšče			
Alsószinevér, *see* Synevyr			
Alsószlatina, *see* Nyžnja Solotvyna			
Alsószlovinka, *see* Nižnie Slovinky			
Alsószvidnik, *see* Nižní Svidník			
Alsótarócz, *see* Nižný Tvarožec			
Alsóvereczke, *see* Nyžni Vorota			
Alsóveresmart, *see* Mala Kopanja			
Alsóvizköz, *see* Nižní Svidník			
Alsóviznicze, *see* Nyžnja Vyznycja			
Alsóvladicsa, *see* Nižná Vladiča			
Andrásháza, *see* Andrijivka			
Andrašovci, *see* Andrijivka, Ung county			

Village	Former Hungarian county or Galician district	Present administrative subdivision	Present country
Andrejivka, *see* Andrzejówka			
Andrejová [Sv] (Andrijova [Ru, U]; Endrevágása [H])	Sáros	Bardejov	Slovakia
Andrejovka [Sv], from 1850 to 1930 and since 1961 part of Orlov			
Andrijivka, Nowy Sącz county, *see* Andrzejówka			
Andrijivka [U] (Andrásháza [H]; Andrašovci [Ru])	Ung	Užhorod	Ukraine
Andrijova, *see* Andrejová			
Andrivka, *see* Andrzejówka			
Andrzejówka [P] (Andrejivka [Ru]; Andrijivka [U]; Adrivka [Ru]; Jedrzejówka [P])	Nowy Sącz	Nowy Sącz	Poland
Antalócz, *see* Antalovci			
Antalovci [Ru, U] (Antalócz [H])	Ung	Užhorod	Ukraine
Apšycja, *see* Vodycja			
Árdánháza, *see* Ardanove			
Ardanove [U] (Árdánháza [H]; Ardanovo [Ru])	Bereg	Iršava	Ukraine
Ardovec', *see* Pidvynohradiv			
Árok, *see* Jarok			
Astrjabik/Astrjabyk, *see* Jastrzębik			
Bábakút, *see* Babyči			
Babyči [Ru, U] (Bábakút [H])	Bereg	Mukačevo	Ukraine
Bachlowa [P] (Bachljava [U]; Bachlova [Ru])	Lesko	Krosno	Poland
Bachlova, *see* Bachlowa			
Bachljava, *see* Bachlowa			
Bačinci, *see* p. 112			
Bačovo, *see* Chabanivka			
Bácskeresztur, *see* Ruski Krstur			
Bacsó, *see* Chabanivka			
Bagniste [P] (Rudavka/Rodavka [Ru]; Rudavka Jaslys'ka [U]; Rudawka Jaśliska [P]) (ceased to exist after 1947)	Sanok	Krosno	Poland
Bagolyháza, *see* Bilasovycja			
Bajerivci, *see* Bajerovce			
Bajerovce [Sv] (Bajerivci [Ru, U]; Bajorvágás [H])	Sáros	Prešov	Slovakia
Bajorvágás, *see* Bajerovce			
Balašovci [Ru, U] (Ballósfalva [H])	Bereg	Mukačevo	Ukraine
Balažijeve, *see* Kuz'myne			
Balázsvágás, *see* Blažov			
Baligrit, *see* Baligród, p. 112			

Village	Former Hungarian county or Galician district	Present administrative subdivision	Present country
Baligród, *see* p. 112			
Ballósfalva, *see* Balašovci			
Balnica [P] (Balnycja [Ru]; Bal'nycja [U])	Lesko	Krosno	Poland
Balnycja/Bal'nycja, *see* Balnica			
Bałucianka [P] (Balutjanka [U]; Bavtjanka [Ru])	Sanok	Krosno	Poland
Balyhorod, *see* Baligród, p. 112			
Banica [P] (Banycja [Ru, U])	Gorlice	Nowy Sącz	Poland
Banica [P] (Banycja [Ru, U])	Grybów	Nowy Sącz	Poland
Banské [Sv] (Banske [Ru]; Bans'ke [U]; Bánszka/Bányapataka [H])	Zemplén	Vranov	Slovakia
Bánszka, *see* Banské			
Bányafalu, *see* Suskove			
Bányafölgy, *see* Duplín			
Bányapataka, *see* Banské			
Banycja, *see* Banica			
Baranya, *see* Baranynci			
**Baranynci [Ru, U] (Baranya [H])	Ung	Užhorod	Ukraine
Barátlak, *see* Rohožník			
Barbovo, *see* Borodivka			
Bárdháza, *see* Borodivka			
Barkóczháza, *see* Ruská Volová			
Barnabás, *see* Kostylivka			
Bártfalva, *see* Dorobratov			
Bartne [P, Ru] (Bortne [Ru, U])	Gorlice	Nowy Sącz	Poland
Barvinok, *see* Barwinek			
Barwinek [P] (Barvinok [Ru, U])	Krosno	Krosno	Poland
Baskócz, *see* Baškovce			
**Baškovce [Sv] (Alsóbaskócz/ Baskócz [H])	Ung	Michalovce	Slovakia
Bátorhegy, *see* Krajná Bystrá			
Bavtjanka, *see* Bałucianka			
Becherov [Sv] (Becheriv [U]; Beheró/Biharó [H])	Sáros	Bardejov	Slovakia
Bedevlja [Ru, U] (Bedőháza [H])	Máramaros	Tjačiv	Ukraine
Bednarka [P] (Bodnarka [Ru, U])	Gorlice	Nowy Sącz	Poland
Bedőháza, *see* Bedevlja			
Begindjatska Pastîl', *see* Behendjats'ka Pastil'			
Behendjats'ka Pastil' [U] (Alsópásztély [H]; Begindjatska Pastîl' [Ru])	Ung	Velykyj Bereznyj	Ukraine
Beheró, *see* Becherov			
Bekrip, *see* Vel'krop			
Bélavézse, *see* Beloveža			
Belchivka/Bełchówka, *see* Borgówka			
Belebovo, *see* Linturovycja			
Belejivci, *see* Belejovce			

Village	Former Hungarian county or Galician district	Present administrative subdivision	Present country
Belejócz, *see* Belejovce			
Belejovce [Sv] (Belejócz [H]; Belejivci [Ru, U])	Sáros	Svidník	Slovakia
Beloveža [Sv] (Bélavézse [H]; Biloveža [Ru, U])	Sáros	Bardejov	Slovakia
**Beňadikovce [Sv] (Benedekvágása/ Bendikóc [H]; Benjadŷkivci [Ru]; Benjadykivci [U])	Sáros	Svidník	Slovakia
*Beňatina [Sv] (Benetine [H]; Benjatyna [Ru, U]; Vadászfalva [H])	Ung	Michalovce	Slovakia
Benedeki, *see* Benedykivci			
Benedekvágása, *see* Beňadikovce			
Benedikóc, *see* Beňadikovce			
Benedykivci [U] (Benedeki [H]; Benedykovci [Ru])	Bereg	Mukačevo	Ukraine
Benetine, *see* Beňatina			
Beniowa [P] (Ben'ova [U]) (ceased to exist after 1947)	Turka	Krosno	Poland
Benjadykivci, *see* Beňadikovce			
Bercsényifalva, *see* Dubrynyč			
Beregbárdos, *see* Bukovec', Bereg			
Beregbükkös, *see* Bukovynka			
Beregfogaras, *see* Fogaraš			
Beregforrás, *see* Rodnykivka			
Bereghalmos, *see* Škurativci			
Beregkisalmás, *see* Zalužžja			
Beregkisfalud, *see* Sil'ce			
Beregkövesd, *see* Kamjans'ke			
Beregleányfalva, *see* Lalove			
Beregnagyalmás, *see* Jabluniv			
Beregpálfalva, *see* Volovycja			
Beregpapfalva, *see* Dilok			
Beregrákos, *see* Rakošyn, p. 113			
Beregrosztoka, *see* Velyka Roztoka			
Beregsárrét, *see* Kal'nyk			
Beregszász, *see* Berehove, p. 112			
Beregszentmiklós, *see* Čynadijeve			
Beregsziklás, *see* Ščerbovec'			
Beregszilvás, *see* Kuz'myne			
Beregszőllős, *see* Lochove			
Berehove, *see* p. 112			
Berehovo, *see* Berehove, p. 112			
Berehy Górne/Horišni, *see* Brzegi Górne			
Bereščajska Vola, *see* Wola Matiaszowa			
Bereska, *see* Berezka			
Berest [P, Ru, U]	Grybów	Nowy Sącz	Poland
Berestiv, *see* Brestov nad Laborcem			

Village	Former Hungarian county or Galician district	Present administrative subdivision	Present country
Berezka [P, U] (Bereska [P, Ru]; Brzozka [P])	Lesko	Krosno	Poland
Bereżki [P] (Berežky [U])	Lesko	Krosno	Poland
Berežky, *see* Bereżki			
Berezna, *see* Berezove			
Bereznek, *see* Bereznyky			
Bereżnica Niżna [P] (Berežnycja Nyžnja [U]) (ceased to exist after 1947)	Lesko	Krosno	Poland
Bereżnica Wyżna [P] (Bereznycja [Ru]; Berežnycja Vyžnja [U])	Lesko	Krosno	Poland
Bereznycja, *see* Bereżnica Wyżna			
Berežnycja Nyžnja, *see* Bereżnica Niżna			
Berežnycja Vyžnja, *see* Bereżnica Wyżna			
Bereznyk, *see* Bereznyky			
Bereznyky [U] (Bereznek [H]; Bereznyk [Ru])	Máramaros	Svaljava	Ukraine
Berezócz, *see* Brezovec			
Berezóka, *see* Brezovka			
Berezova, *see* Brzezowa			
Berezove [U] (Berezna [H]; Berezovo [Ru])	Máramaros	Chust	Ukraine
Berezovec', Zemplén district, *see* Brezovec			
Berezovec/Berezovec', Lesko district, *see* Brzozowiec			
Berezovo, *see* Berezove			
Berezowiec, *see* Brzozowiec			
Berkasovo, *see* p. 112			
Berkenyéd, *see* Jarabina			
Berlebaš, *see* Kostylivka			
Besko [P] (Bos'ko [Ru, U])	Sanok	Krosno	Poland
Biała Woda [P] (Bila Voda [Ru, U])	Nowy Targ	Nowy Sącz	Poland
Bielanka [P] (Bilanka [Ru]; Biljanka [U])	Gorlice	Nowy Sącz	Poland
Bieliczna [P] (Bilična [Ru]; Bylyčna [U]) (ceased to exist after 1947)	Grybów	Nowy Sącz	Poland
Biharó, *see* Becherov			
Bila Voda, *see* Biała Woda			
Bilanka, *see* Bielanka			
Bilasovycja [Ru, U] (Bagolyháza [H])	Bereg	Volovec'	Ukraine
Bil'careva, *see* Binczarowa			
Bilična, *see* Bieliczna			
Bilin, *see* Bilyn			
Biljanka, *see* Bielanka			
Bilke, *see* Bilky			
Bilky [Ru, U] (Bilke [H])	Bereg	Iršava	Ukraine
Bilovarci [U] (Bilovarec' [Ru]; Kiskirva [H])	Máramaros	Tjačiv	Ukraine
Bilovarec', *see* Bilovarci			

Village	Former Hungarian county or Galician district	Present administrative subdivision	Present country
Biloveža, *see* Beloveža			
Bilŷj Potok, *see* Dilove			
Bilyn [Ru, U] (Bilin [H])	Máramaros	Rachiv	Ukraine
Binczarowa [P] (Bil'careva [U]; Bolcarjova/Borcalova [Ru])	Grybów	Nowy Sącz	Poland
Bistra [U] (Bŷstrŷj [Ru]; Petrovabisztra [H])	Máramaros	Maramureş	Romania
Blažov [Sv] (Balázsvágás [H]; Blaživ [Ru, U]) (ceased to exist in 1950)	Sáros	Prešov	Slovakia
Blechnarka [P] (Blichnarka [Ru, U])	Gorlice	Nowy Sącz	Poland
Blichnarka, *see* Blechnarka			
Bobovyšče [U] (Bobovyšči [Ru]; Borhalom [H])	Bereg	Mukačevo	Ukraine
Bochivka, *see* Borgówka			
Bociocoiu [Ro] (Bočkov [Ru]; Byčkiv [U]; Nagybocskó [H])	Máramaros	Maramureş	Romania
Bočkov, *see* Bociocoiu			
Bodaki [P] (Bodaky [Ru, U])	Gorlice	Nowy Sącz	Poland
Bodaky, *see* Bodaki			
Bodnarka, *see* Bednarka			
Bodružal' [Sv] (Bodružal [Ru, U]; Rózsadomb [H])	Sáros	Svidník	Slovakia
Bodzás, *see* Bžany			
Bogdány, *see* Bohdan			
Boglárka, *see* Bogliarka			
Bogliarka [Sv] (Boglárka [H, Ru]; Bohljarka [U])	Sáros	Bardejov	Slovakia
Bogusza [P] (Boguša [Ru]; Bohuša [U])	Grybów	Nowy Sącz	Poland
Boharevycja [U] (Boharovycja [Ru]; Falucska [H])	Bereg	Iršava	Ukraine
Bohdan [Ru, U] (Bogdány/ Tiszabogdány [H])	Máramaros	Rachiv	Ukraine
Bohuša, *see* Bogusza			
**Bokša [Ru, Sv, U]	Zemplén	Svidník	Slovakia
Bolcarjova, *see* Binczarowa			
Bölcsős, *see* Kolibabovce			
Bonarivka, *see* Bonarówka			
Bonarówka [P] (Bonarivka [U])	Rzeszów	Rzeszów	Poland
Borcalova, *see* Binczarowa			
Borgówka [P] (Belchivka [U]; Bełchowka [P]; Bochivka [Ru]) (ceased to exist after 1947)	Sanok	Krosno	Poland
Borhalom, *see* Bobovyšče			
Borkút, *see* Kvasy			
Boró, *see* Borov			
Boród, *see* Brid			

Village	Former Hungarian county or Galician district	Present administrative subdivision	Present country
Borodivka [U] (Barbovo [Ru]; Bárdháza [H])	Bereg	Mukačevo	Ukraine
Borókás, *see* Jedlinka			
Borosnya, *see* Brusnica			
Borov [Sv] (Boró [H]; Boriv [Ru, U]), since 1970 part of Medzilaborce			
Borsučyna [Ru, U] (Borzfalva [H])	Bereg	Volovec'	Ukraine
Bortne, *see* Bartne			
Boržavs'ke [U] Nagycsongova [H]; Velyka Čengava [Ru]; Velyka Čynhava [U])	Ugocsa	Vynohradiv	Ukraine
Borzfalva, *see* Borsučyna			
Bos'ko, *see* Besko			
Brestiv [U] (Brestov [Ru]; Ormód [H])	Bereg	Mukačevo	Ukraine
Brestov, *see* Brestiv			
Brestov nad Laborcom [Sv] (Berestiu [Ru]; Berestiv [U]; Laborczbér [H])	Zemplen	Humenné	Slovakia
Breznička [Ru, Sv] (Breznyčka [U]; Kisberezsnye [H])	Zemplén	Svidník	Slovakia
Brezovec [Sv] (Berezócz [H]; Berezovec' [U])	Zemplén	Humenné	Slovakia
Brezovka [Sv] (Berezóka [H])	Sáros	Bardejov	Slovakia
Brid [U] (Boród [H]; Brod [Ru])	Bereg	Iršava	Ukraine
Brod, *see* Brid			
Brunarja Nyžnja, *see* Brunary Niżne			
Brunarja Vyšnja, *see* Brunary Wyżne			
Brunary Niżne [P] (Brunarja Nyžnja [Ru]; Brunary Nyžni [U])	Grybów	Nowy Sącz	Poland
Brunary Wyżne [P] (Brunarja Vyšnja [Ru]; Brunary Vyžni [U])	Grybów	Nowy Sącz	Poland
Brusnica [Ru, Sv] (Borosnya [H]; Brusnycja [U]; Brusnyicza [H])	Zemplén	Svidník	Slovakia
Brusnycja, *see* Brusnica			
Brusnyicza, *see* Brusnica			
Brustov [Ru, U] (Lombos [H])	Bereg	Svaljava	Ukraine
Brusturŷ, *see* Lopuchiv			
Brusztura, *see* Lopuchiv			
Brzegi Górne [P] (Berehy Górne [P]; Berehy Horišni [U])	Lesko	Krosno	Poland
Brezova, *see* Brzezowa			
Brzezowa [P] (Berezova [Ru, U]; Brezova [Ru])	Jasło	Krosno	Poland
Brzozka, *see* Berezka			
Brzozowiec [P] (Berezovec [Ru]; Berezovec' [U]; Berezowiec [P])	Lesko	Krosno	Poland
Buk [P, U]	Lesko	Krosno	Poland

Village	Former Hungarian county or Galician district	Present administrative subdivision	Present country
Bukivceve [U] (Bukovc'ova [Ru]; Bükkös/Ungbükkös [H])	Ung	Velykyj Bereznyj	Ukraine
Bukivci, *see* Bukovce			
Bükkös, Bereg county, *see* Bukovynka			
Bükkös, Ung county, *see* Bukivceve			
Bükköspatak, *see* Bukovec', Máramaros county			
Bukócz, *see* Bukovec', Bereg county			
Bukovce [Sv] (Bukivci [U])	Zemplén	Svidník	Slovakia
Bukovc'ova, *see* Bukivceve			
Bukovec' [Ru, U] (Beregbárdos/Bukócz [H])	Bereg	Volovec'	Ukraine
Bukovec' [Ru, U] (Bükköspatak [H])	Máramaros	Mižhirja	Ukraine
Bukovec', Lesko county, *see* Bukowiec			
Bukovec', Turka county, *see* Bukowiec			
Bukovynka [Ru, U] (Beregbükkös/Bükkös [H])	Bereg	Mukačevo	Ukraine
Bukowiec [P] (Bukovec' [U]) (ceased to exist after 1947)	Lesko	Krosno	Poland
Bukowiec [P] (Bukovec' [U])	Turka	Krosno	Poland
Bustyaháza, *see* Buštyna			
Buštyna [U] (Bustyaháza [H]; Bužčyno [Ru])	Máramaros	Tjačiv	Ukraine
Byčkiv, *see* Bocicoiu			
Bylyčna, *see* Bieliczna			
Bystrá [Sv] (Bŷstra [Ru]; Hegyesbisztra/Sztropkóbisztra [H])	Zemplén	Svidník	Slovakia
Bystre [P, U] (Bŷstrŷj [Ru])	Lesko	Krosno	Poland
Bystrycja [U] (Repede [H]; Rjapid' [Ru])	Bereg	Mukačevo	Ukraine
Bystryj [U] (Bŷstrŷj [Ru]; Sebesfalva [H])	Bereg	Volovec'	Ukraine
Bŷstrŷj, Lesko district, *see* Bystre			
Bŷstrŷj, Máramaros county, *see* Bistra			
Bŷstrŷj, Ung county, *see* Verchovyna-Bystra			
**Bžany [Sv, U] (Bodzás [H]; Bzanŷ [Ru])	Zemplén	Svidník	Slovakia
Čabalivci, *see* Čabalovce			
Čabalovce [Sv] (Čabalivci [Ru, U]; Csabalócz és Sterkócz [H])	Zemplén	Humenné	Slovakia
Čabiny [Sv] (Čabyny [U])	Zemplén	Medzilaborce	Slovakia
Čabyny, *see* Čabiny			
Čapovci, *see* Čopivci			
Čarna, *see* Czarna			
Čarna Voda, *see* Czarna Woda			
Čarne, *see* Czarne			
Čarnŷj, *see* Czarne			
Caryns'ke, *see* Caryńskie			
Caryńskie [P] (Caryns'ke [U]) (ceased to exist after 1947)	Lesko	Krosno	Poland
Čašyn, *see* Czaszyn			
Čejšyn, *see* Czaszyn			

Village	Former Hungarian county or Galician district	Present administrative subdivision	Present country
Čerejivci [U] (Čerejovci [Ru]; Czerház [H])	Bereg	Mukačevo	Ukraine
Čerejovci, *see* Čerejivci			
Čeremcha, *see* Czeremcha			
Cernina [Sv] (Cernyna [U]; Cernynŷ [Ru]; Czernina/Felsőcsernye [H])	Sáros	Svidník	Slovakia
Cernyna, *see* Cernina			
Cernynŷ, *see* Cernina			
Čertež, Sanok district, *see* Czerteż			
Čertež, Ung county, *see* Čertez			
Čertiž, Sanok district, *see* Czerteż			
Čertiž [U] (Čertež [Ru]; Czertész/ Ungczertész [H])	Ung	Užhorod	Ukraine
Čertižné [Sv] (Čertižne [Ru, U]; Csertész/Nagycsertész [H])	Zemplén	Humenné	Slovakia
Čertyžne, *see* Czertyżne			
Červeneve [U] (Červen'ovo [Ru]; Czerlenő [H])	Bereg	Mukačevo	Ukraine
Červen'ovo, *see* Červeneve			
Češyn, *see* Czaszyn			
Chabanivka [U] (Bačovo [Ru]; Bacsó [H])	Ung	Užhorod	Ukraine
Chlumec', *see* Cholmec'			
Chmel'ová [Sv] (Chmel'ova [Ru, U]; Komlósa/Komlóspatak [H])	Sáros	Bardejov	Slovakia
Chmil'nyk [Ru, U] (Komlós [H]; Komluš [Ru])	Bereg	Iršava	Ukraine
Choceń [P] (Chotin' [U]) (ceased to exist after 1947)	Lesko	Krosno	Poland
Cholmec' [U (Chlumec' [Ru]; Homlőcz [H])	Ugocsa	Vynohradiv	Ukraine
Chon'kivci, *see* Choňkovce			
Choňkovce [Sv] (Alsóhunkócz [H]; Chon'kivci [U]; Hunkócz [H])	Ung	Michalovce	Slovakia
Chotin', *see* Choceń			
Chudl'ove [U] (Chudl'ovo [Ru]; Horlyó [H])	Ung	Užhorod	Ukraine
Chudl'ovo, *see* Chudl'ove			
Chust [Ru, U] (Huszt [H])	Máramaros	Chust	Ukraine
Chyrowa [P] (Hyrova [Ru, U]; Hyrowa [P])	Krosno	Krosno	Poland
Chyža [U] (Chyži [Ru]; Kistarna/Tarna [H])	Ugocsa	Vynohradiv	Ukraine
Chyzi, *see* Chyža			
Cichania, *see* Ciechania			
Ciechania [P] (Cichania [P]; Tychanja [Ru, U]) (ceased to exist after 1947)	Krosno	Krosno	Poland
Cigel'ka [Sv] (Cigolka [Ru]; Cyhelka [U]; Czigelka [H])	Sáros	Bardejov	Slovakia
Cigla [Ru, Sv] (Cyhlja [U]; Czigla [H])	Sáros	Svidník	Slovakia
Cigolka, *see* Cigel'ka			
Činjad'ovo, *see* Čynadijeve			

Village	Former Hungarian county or Galician district	Present administrative subdivision	Present country
Čirč [Ru, Sv] (Csércs [H]; Čyrč [U])	Sáros	Stará L'ubovňa	Slovakia
Cisna [P] (Tisna [Ru, U])	Lesko	Krosno	Poland
Cisowiec [P] (Tysovec [Ru]; Tysivec' [U])	Lesko	Krosno	Poland
Čoma [Ru, U] (Čuma [Ru])	Ugocsa	Berehovo	Ukraine
Čomal'ovo, *see* Čumaleve			
Čopivci [U] (Čapovci [Ru]; Csapolcz [H])	Bereg	Mukačevo	Ukraine
Čorna [Ru, U] (Csamatő/Csomafalva [H])	Ugocsa	Vynohradiv	Ukraine
Čorna Voda, *see* Czarna Woda			
Čorne, Gorlice county, *see* Czarne			
Čorne, Sáros county, *see* Šarišské Čierné			
Čornoholova [Ru, U] (Sóhát [H])	Ung	Velykyj Bereznyj	Ukraine
Čornorky, *see* Czarnorzeki			
Čornyj Potik [U] (Čornŷj Potok [Ru]; Kenézpatak [H])	Bereg	Iršava	Ukraine
Crăciuneşti, *see* p. 112			
Csabaháza, *see* Čabalovce			
Csabalócz és Sterkocz, *see* Čabalovce			
Csapolcz, *see* Čopovci			
Csamatő, *see* Čorna			
Csarnó, *see* Šarišské Čierné			
Csendes, *see* Tyšiv			
Csendespatak, *see* Tichý Potok			
Csércs, *see* Čirč			
Cseres, *see* Dubová			
Csergőzávod, *see* Závadka, Sáros county			
Cserhalom, *see* Dibrivka, Bereg county			
Cserjés, *see* Lozjans'kyj			
Csertész, Ung county, *see* Čertiž			
Csertész, Zemplén county, *see* Čertižné			
Csillagfalva, *see* Knjahynja			
Csomafalva, *see* Čorna			
Csománfalva, *see* Čumaleve			
Csontos, *see* Kostryna			
Csukaháza, *see* Čukalovce			
Csuszka, *see* Tjuška			
Čukalivci, *see* Čukalovce			
Čukalovce [Sv] (Csukaháza [H]; Čukalivci [Ru, U])	Zemplén	Humenné	Slovakia
Čuma, *see* Čoma			
Čumaleve [U] (Čomal'ovo [Ru]; Csománfalva [H])	Máramaros	Tjačiv	Ukraine
Cŷganovci, *see* Cyhanivci			
Cyhanivci [U] (Cŷganovci [Ru]; Czigányos [H])	Ung	Užhorod	Ukraine
Cyhelka, *see* Cigel'ka			
Cyhlja, *see* Cigla			

Village	Former Hungarian county or Galician district	Present administrative subdivision	Present country
Čynadijeve [U] (Beregszentmiklós [H]; Činjad'ovo [Ru]; Szentmiklós [H])	Bereg	Mukačevo	Ukraine
Čyrč, *see* Čirč			
Čyrna, *see* Czyrna			
Čystohorb, *see* Górna Wieś			
Czarna [P] (Čarna [Ru, U])	Grybów	Nowy Sącz	Poland
Czarna Woda [P] (Čarna Voda [Ru]; Čorna Voda [U])	Nowy Targ	Nowy Sącz	Poland
Czarne [P] (Čarne/Čarnŷj [Ru]; Čorne [Ru, U])	Gorlice	Nowy Sącz	Poland
Czarnorzeki [P] (Čornoky [U])	Krosno	Krosno	Poland
Czaszyn [P] (Čašyn [U]; Čejšyn/ Češyn [Ru])	Sanok	Krosno	Poland
Czeremcha [P] (Čeremcha [Ru, U]) (ceased to exist after 1947)	Sanok	Krosno	Poland
Czerház, *see* Čerejivci			
Czerlenő, *see* Červeneve			
Czernina, *see* Cernina			
Czerteż [P] (Čertež [U]; Čertiž [Ru])	Sanok	Krosno	Poland
Czertyżne [P] (Čertyžne [Ru, U])	Grybów	Nowy Sącz	Poland
Cziganyos, *see* Cyhanivci			
Czigelka, *see* Cigel'ka			
Czigla, *see* Cigla			
Czirókaófalu, *see* Starina, Zemplén county			
Czyrna [P] (Čyrna [Ru, U])	Grybów	Nowy Sącz	Poland
Czystogarb/Czystohorb, *see* Górna Wieś			
Dąbrówka Ruska [P] (Dubrivka [Ru]; Dubrivka Rus'ka [U])	Sanok	Krosno	Poland
Dadafalva, *see* Dedačov			
Daliowa [P] (Dalova [Ru]; Dal'ova [U])	Sanok	Krosno	Poland
Dalova/Dal'ova, *see* Daliowa			
Danylove [U] (Danylovo [Ru]; Husztófalva [H])	Máramaros	Chust	Ukraine
Danylovo, *see* Danylove			
Dara [Ru, Sv, U] (since 1980 ceased to exist)	Zemplén	Humenné	Slovakia
Dariv, *see* Darów			
Darócz, *see* Dravci			
Darov, *see* Darów			
Darów [P] (Dariv [Ru, U]; Darov [Ru]) (ceased to exist after 1947)	Sanok	Krosno	Poland
Darva, *see* Kolodne, Máramaros county			
Dávidfalva, *see* Zavydove			
Davidov [Sv] (Dávidvágása [H]; Davŷdiv [Ru]; Davydiv [U])	Zemplén	Vranov	Slovakia
Dávidvágása, *see* Davidov			
Davydiv/Davŷdiv, *see* Davidov			

Village	Former Hungarian county or Galician district	Present administrative subdivision	Present country
**Dedačov [Sv] (Dadafalva/Dedasócz [H]; Didačiv [Ru]; Dydačiv [U])	Zemplén	Humenné	Slovakia
Dedasócz, *see* Dedačov			
Dengláz, *see* Denkovci			
*Denkovci [Ru] (Dengláz [H]), since 1920 part of Velyki Lazy			
Dér, *see* Mrazovce			
Deskófalva, *see* Deškovycja			
Deškovycja [Ru, U] (Deskófalva [H])	Bereg	Iršava	Ukraine
Desno, *see* Deszno			
Desznica [P] (Došnycja [Ru, U])	Jasło	Krosno	Poland
Deszno [P] (Desno [Ru]; Došno [U])	Sanok	Krosno	Poland
Detre, *see* Detrík			
Detrík [Sv] (Detre [H]; Detryk [Ru, U])	Zemplén	Vranov	Slovakia
Detryk, *see* Detrík			
Dibrivka [U] (Cserhalom [H]; Dubrovka and Boržavoju [Ru]; Tölgyes [H])	Bereg	Iršava	Ukraine
Dibrivka [U] (Dubrovka [Ru]; Ungtölgyes [H])	Ung	Užhorod	Ukraine
Dibrova, *see* p. 112			
Didačiv, *see* Dedačov			
Dilok [Ru, U] (Beregpapfalva/Papfalva [H])	Bereg	Mukačevo	Ukraine
Dilok [Ru, U]	Máramaros	Chust	Ukraine
Dilove [U] (Bîlŷj Potok [Ru]; Fejérpatak/ Terebesfejérpatak [H]; Trebušany [Ru])	Máramaros	Rachiv	Ukraine
Diskovycja, *see* Dyskovycja			
Djurd'ov, *see* Djurdjevo, p. 112			
Djurdjevo, *see* p. 112			
Dlhoňa [Sv] (Dohun' [U]; Dolgonya [H])	Sáros	Svidník	Slovakia
Długie [P] (Dovhe [Ru, U]; Dovhŷ [Ru]) (ceased to exist after 1947)	Gorlice	Nowy Sącz	Poland
Dobrians'ke [U] (Njagovo [Ru]; Nyágova [H])	Máramaros	Tjačiv	Ukraine
Dobroslava [Ru, Sv, U] (Dobroszló [H])	Sáros	Svidník	Slovakia
Dobroszló, *see* Dobroslava			
Dohun', *see* Dlhoňa			
Dolgonya, *see* Dlhoňa			
Dolha, *see* Dovhe			
Dolina [P] (Dolyna [U])	Sanok	Krosno	Poland
Dolyna, *see* Dolina			
Dołżyca [P] (Dolżycja [U]; Dovžycja [Ru, U])	Sanok	Krosno	Poland
Dołżyca [P] (Dołżyce [P]; Dolżycja [Ru, U]; Dovžycja [U])	Lesko	Krosno	Poland
Dołżyce, *see* Dołżyca, Lesko district			
Dolżycja, *see* Dołżyca, Lesko district; Sanok district			
Domafalva, *see* Domašyn			
Domanynci [Ru, U] (Alsódomonya [H])	Ung	Užhorod	Ukraine

Village	Former Hungarian county or Galician district	Present administrative subdivision	Present country

Kisbukócz, *see* Malé Bukovce
Kiscserjés, *see* Linturovycja
Kiscsongova, *see* Zavadka, Ugocsa county
Kisderencs, *see* Malá Driečna
Kisfagyalos, *see* Svidnička
Kisfalud, *see* Sil'ce
Kisgereblyés, *see* Hrabová Roztoka
Kisgombás, *see* Gribov
Kisgyertyános, *see* Vyšný Hrabovec
Kishárs, *see* Malý Lypník
Kishidvég, *see* Pasika
Kishollód, *see* Havranec
Kiskereszt, *see* Kríže
Kiskirva, *see* Bilovarci
Kiskökény, *see* Trnkov
Kiskolon, *see* Kolonica
Kiskőrösfő, *see* Okružná
Kiskurima, *see* Kurimka
Kisléczfalva, *see* Lecovycja
Kislipnik, *see* Malý Lipník
Kismedvés, *see* Medvedzie
Kismező, *see* Valea Vişeului
Kismihály, *see* Michajlov
Kismogyorós, *see* Mykulivci
Kisolysó, *see* Olšavka
Kispálos, *see* Pavlove
Kispásztély, *see* Pastil'ky
Kispatak, *see* Rička
Kispereszlő, *see* Príslop
Kispetőfalva, *see* Petejovce
Kispolány, *see* Malá Pol'ana
Kisrákócz, *see* Malyj Rakovec'
Kisrétfalu, *see* Novoselycja, Bereg county
Kisrosztoka, *see* Vyšnja Roztoka
Kissarkad, *see* Šarkad'
Kisszabados, *see* Rus'ká Vol'a
Kisszolyva, *see* Skotars'ke
Kistarna, *see* Chyža
Kistavas, *see* Malé Staškovce
Kistölgyes, *see* Dúbrava
Kistopolya, *see* Topol'a
Kisturjaszög, *see* Turyčky
Kisvadas, *see* Dyskovycja
Kisvajszló, *see* Vislava
Kisvalkó, *see* Valkov
Kisvölgy, *see* Krišlovce
Kjaton'/Kjatonja, *see* Kwiatoń

Village	Former Hungarian county or Galician district	Present administrative subdivision	Present country
Klacsanó, *see* Kljačanove			
Klastromalja, *see* Pidmonastyr			
Klembarok, *see* Klenov			
Klembérk, *see* Klenov			
Klenov [Sv] (Kelembér [H]; Klembarok [Sv]; Klembérk [H])	Sáros	Prešov	Slovakia
Klenová [Sv] (Kelen [H]; Klenova [Ru, U])	Zemplén	Humenné	Slovakia
Klimkówka [P] (Klymkivka [Ru, U])	Gorlice	Nowy Sącz	Poland
Kljačanove [U] (Klacsanó [H]; Klyčanovo [Ru])	Bereg	Mukačevo	Ukraine
Ključarky [Ru, U] (Kulcsa/Várkulcsa [H])	Bereg	Mukačevo	Ukraine
Kl'očky [Ru, U] (Lakatosfalva [H])	Bereg	Mukačevo	Ukraine
Klokočov [Sv] (Hajagos [H]; Klokočovo [Ru])	Ung	Michalovce	Slovakia
Klopitnycja, *see* Kłopotnica			
Kłopotnica [P] (Klopitnycja [U]; Kvopitnycja [Ru])	Jasło	Krosno	Poland
Klyčanovo, *see* Kljačanove			
Klymkivka, *see* Klimkówka			
Knjahynja [U] (Csillagfalva [H]; Knjahynyn [Ru])	Ung	Velykyj Bereznyj	Ukraine
Kobalevycja [U] (Gálfalva [H]; Kobalovycja [Ru])	Bereg	Iršava	Ukraine
Kobalovycja, *see* Kobalevycja			
Kobivci, *see* Kolbovce			
Köblér, *see* Kybljary			
Kobulnicza, *see* Kobylnice			
Kobylec'ka Poljana, *see* p. 112			
Kobŷljarŷ, *see* Kybljary			
**Kobylnice [Sv] (Kabalas/ Kobulnicza [H]; Kobŷl'nica [Ru]; Kobylnycja [U])	Sáros	Bardejov	Slovakia
Kocur, *see* Kucura			
Koczkaszállás, *see* Kosyne			
Kokény, *see* Trnkov			
Kökényes, *see* Ternove			
Kokyňa, *see* Trnkov			
Kolbasov [Sv] (Kovbasiv [U]; Kovbasuv [Ru]; Koves/Végaszó [H])	Zemplén	Humenné	Slovakia
Kolbivci, *see* Kolbovce			
Kolbovce [Sv] (Kobivci [Ru]; Kolbivci [U])	Zemplén	Svidník	Slovakia
Kolcsény, *see* Kol'čyne			
Kol'čyne [U] (Kolcsény [H]; Kolčyno [Ru])	Bereg	Mukačevo	Ukraine
Kolčyno, *see* Kol'čyne			
Kolibabovce [Sv] (Bölcsős [H])	Ung	Michalovce	Slovakia
Koločava [Ru, U] (Alsókalocsa [H])	Máramaros	Mižhirja	Ukraine

Village	Former Hungarian county or Galician district	Present administrative subdivision	Present country
Kolodne [U] (Kolodnoje [Ru]; Tökesfalu [H])	Bereg	Iršava	Ukraine
Kolodne [U] (Darva [H]; Kolodnoje [Ru])	Máramaros	Tjačiv	Ukraine
Kolodnoje, *see* Kolodne, Bereg county; Máramaros county			
Kolonica [Ru, Sv] (Kiskolon [H]; Kolonycja [U])	Zemplén	Humenné	Slovakia
Kołonice [P] (Kolonyci [Ru, U])	Lesko	Krosno	Poland
Kolonyci, *see* Kołonice			
Kolonycja, *see* Kolonica			
Koman'ča, *see* Komańcza			
Komańcza [P] (Koman'ča [Ru, U]; Kumanča [Ru])	Sanok	Krosno	Poland
Komját, *see* Velyki Komjaty			
Komlós, *see* Chmil'nyk			
Komlósa, *see* Chmel'ová			
Komlóspatak, *see* Chmel'ová			
Komluš, *see* Chmil'nyk			
Konečna, *see* Konieczna			
Konieczna [P] (Konečna [Ru, U])	Gorlice	Nowy Sącz	Poland
Konjuš, *see* Koňuš			
Konoplivci [U] (Kendereske [H]; Kenderešov [Ru])	Bereg	Mukačevo	Ukraine
Końskie [P] (Kins'kie [U])	Brzozów	Krosno	Poland
Koňuš [Sv] (Konjuš [U] Unglovasd [H])	Ung	Michalovce	Slovakia
Kopár, *see* Rosoš			
Kopašneve [U] (Gernyés [H]; Kopašnovo [Ru])	Máramaros	Chust	Ukraine
Kopašnovo, *see* Kopašneve			
Kőporuba, *see* Kamenná Poruba			
Kopynivci [U] (Kopynovci [Ru]; Mogyorós/Nagymogyorós [H])	Bereg	Mukačevo	Ukraine
Kopynovci, *see* Kopynivci			
Korejivci, *see* Korejovce			
Korejócz, *see* Korejovce			
Korejovce [Sv] (Korejivci [Ru, U]; Korejócz/Korócz [H])	Sáros	Svidník	Slovakia
Körmös, *see* Kožuchovce			
Korócz, *see* Korejovce			
Koroleva Rus'ka, *see* Królowa Górna			
Koroleve [U] (Királyháza [H]; Kral'ovo nad Tysoju [Ru])	Ugocsa	Vynohradiv	Ukraine
Korolyk Volos'kyj, *see* Królik Wołoski			
**Koroml'a [U] (Koromlak/ Korumlya [H])	Ung	Michalovce	Slovakia
Koromlak, *see* Koroml'a			
Körösény, *see* Krušinec			

Village	Former Hungarian county or Galician district	Present administrative subdivision	Present country
Kőrösfő, *see* Okružná			
Kőrősmező, *see* Jasynja			
Korosten'ka, *see* Krasna, Krosno county			
Körtvélyes, *see* Hrušove			
Korumlya, *see* Koroml'a			
Korunková [Sv] (Korunkova [Ru, U]; Puczák/Pusztaháza [H])	Zemplén	Svidník	Slovakia
*Korytnjany [U] (Kereknye [H]; Korŷtnjanŷ [Ru])	Ung	Užhorod	Ukraine
Košeleve [U] (Keselymező [H]; Košel'ovo [Ru])	Máramaros	Chust	Ukraine
Košel'ovo, *see* Košeleve			
Kosivs'ka Poljana [U] (Kaszómező [H]; Kosovska Poljana [Ru])	Máramaros	Rachiv	Ukraine
Kosovska Poljana, *see* Kosivs'ka Poljana			
Kostarivci, *see* Kostarowce			
Kostarowce [P] (Kostarivci [U])	Sanok	Krosno	Poland
Kost'ova Pastil' [Ru, U] (Nagypásztély [H])	Ung	Velykyj Bereznyj	Ukraine
Kostryna [Ru, U] (Csontos [H])	Ung	Velykyj Bereznyj	Ukraine
Kostylivka [U] (Barnabás [H]; Berlebaš [Ru])	Máramaros	Rachiv	Ukraine
Kosyne [U] (Koczkaszállás [H]; Kosyno [Ru])	Bereg	Mukačevo	Ukraine
Kosyno, *see* Kosyne			
Kotań [P] (Kotan [Ru]; Kotan' [U])	Jasło	Krosno	Poland
Kőtelep, *see* Kružlov			
Kotel'nycja [Ru, U] (Katlanfalu [H])	Bereg	Volovec'	Ukraine
Kotiv, *see* Kotów			
Kotów [P] (Kotiv [Ru, U])	Nowy Sącz	Nowy Sącz	Poland
Kovácsrét, *see* Kušnycja			
Kővágó, *see* Kamenná Poruba			
Kovászó, *see* Kvasove			
Kovbasiv/Kovbasuv, *see* Kolbasov			
Kovbivci, *see* Kolbovce			
Köves, *see* Kolbovce			
Kövesd, *see* Kamjans'ke			
Kövesfalva, *see* Kamienka			
Kövesliget, *see* Drahove			
Kožany [Sv, U] (Kozsány [H])	Sáros	Bardejov	Slovakia
Kozsány, *see* Kožany			
Kozsuhócz, *see* Kožuchovce			
Kožuchivci, *see* Kožuchovce			
Kožuchovce [Sv] (Körmös/Kozsuhócz [H]; Kožuchivci [Ru, U])	Sáros	Svidník	Slovakia
Kožuszne [P] (Kožušne [U])	Sanok	Krosno	Poland

Village	Former Hungarian county or Galician district	Present administrative subdivision	Present country
Lukova, *see* Lukove			
Lukove [U] (Lukova [H]; Lukovo [Ru])	Bereg	Iršava	Ukraine
Lukove, Lesko district, *see* Łukowe			
Łukowe [P] (Lukiv [Ru]; Lukove [U])	Lesko	Krosno	Poland
Lukovo, *see* Lukove, Bereg county			
Lunca la Tisa [Ro] (Lonka [H])	Máramaros	Maramureş	Romania
Lupkiv, *see* Łupków			
Łupków [P] (Lupkiv [U])	Lesko	Krosno	Poland
L'utina [Sv] (Litinye [H]; Ljutyna [U])	Sáros	Prešov	Slovakia
Lypča [Ru, U] (Lipcse [H])	Máramaros	Chust	Ukraine
Lypec'ka Poljana [Ru, U] (Lipesemező/ Lipcse Polyána [H])	Máramaros	Chust	Ukraine
Lypna, *see* Lipna			
Lypova, *see* Lipová			
Lypovec/Lypovec, Sanok district *see* Lipowiec			
Lypovec' [Ru, U] (Hárs [H])	Ung	Perečyn	Ukraine
Lysyčeve [U] (Lysyčovo [Ru]; Rókamező [H])	Máramaros	Iršava	Ukraine
Lysyčovo, *see* Lysyčeve			
Lytmanova, *see* Litmanová			
Maciejowa [P] (Macjova [Ru]; Matijeva [U])	Nowy Sącz	Nowy Sącz	Poland
Macina Velyka, *see* Męcina Wielka			
Macjova, *see* Maciejowa			
Macyna Velyka, *see* Męcina Wielka			
Magyarkomját, *see* Velyki Komjaty			
Majdan [P,U] (Sviržova Rus'ka [Ru, U]; Sviržova [Ru]; Świerżowa Ruśka [P]) (ceased to exist after 1947)	Jasło	Krosno	Poland
Majdan [P, U]	Lesko	Krosno	Poland
Majdan [Ru, U] (Majdánka [H])	Máramaros	Mižhirja	Ukraine
Majdánka, *see* Majdan, Máramaros county			
Makarja, *see* Makar'ove			
Makarjovo, *see* Makar'ove			
Makar'ove [U] (Makarja [H]; Makarjovo [Ru])	Bereg	Mukačevo	Ukraine
Makivci, *see* Makovce			
Makócz, *see* Makovce			
Mákos, *see* Makovce			
Makovce [Sv] (Makivci [Ru, U]; Makócz/ Mákos [H])	Zemplén	Svidník	Slovakia
Mala Čengava, *see* Zavadka, Ugocsa county			
Mala Drična, *see* Malá Diečna			
Malá Driečna [Sv] (Kisderencs [H]; Mala Drična [Ru, U]; Zempléndricsna [H]), since 1960 part of Vladiča			

Village	Former Hungarian county or Galician district	Present administrative subdivision	Present country
Mala Kopanja [Ru, U] (Alsóveresmart [H])	Ugocsa	Vynohradiv	Ukraine
Mala Martynka [Ru, U] (Mártonka [H])	Bereg	Svaljava	Ukraine
Malá Pol'ana [Sv] (Kispolány [H]; Mala Poljana [Ru, U]; Sztropkópolena [H])	Zemplén	Svidník	Slovakia
Mala Poljana, *see* Malá Pol'ana			
Mala Roztoka [U] (Roztoka [Ru]; Szőllősrosztoka [H])	Ugocsa	Iršava	Ukraine
Malastiv, *see* Małastów			
Małastów [P] (Malastiv [U]; Mavastiv [Ru])	Gorlice	Nowy Sącz	Poland
Malcov [Ru, Sv, U] (Malczó [H])	Sáros	Bardejov	Slovakia
Malczó, *see* Malcov			
Malé Bukovce [Sv] (Kisbukócz [H]; Malyj Bukovec' [U]; Malŷj Bukovec [Ru]; Zemplénbukócz [H]), since 1964 part of Bukovce			
Malé Staškovce [Sv] (Kistavas [H]; Mali Staškivci [U]; Malŷ Staškivci [Ru]; Zemplénsztaskócz [H]), part of Staškovce			
Mali Staškivci, *see* Malé Staškovce			
Malmos, *see* Strojne			
Malý Lipník [Sv] (Kishárs/Kislipnik [H]; Malŷj Lipnik [Ru]; Malyj Lypnyk [U])	Sáros	Stará L'ubovňa	Slovakia
Malŷ Staškivci, *see* Malé Staškovce			
Malý Sulín [Sv] (Malyj Sulyn [U]; Malŷj Sulin [Ru]; Szulin [H]), since 1961 part of Sulín			
Malyj Bereznyj [U] (Kisberezna [H]; Malŷj Bereznŷj [Ru])	Ung	Velykyj Bereznyj	Ukraine
Malyj Bukovec', *see* Malé Bukovce			
Malŷj Lipnik, *see* Malý Lipník			
Malyj Lypnyk, *see* Malý Lipník			
Malyj Rakovec' [U] (Kisrákócz [H]; Malŷj Rakovec' [Ru])	Ugocsa	Iršava	Ukraine
Malŷj Sulin, *see* Malý Sulín			
Malyj Sulyn, *see* Malý Sulín			
Maniów [P] (Maniv [U])	Lesko	Krosno	Poland
Maniv, *see* Maniów			
Máramarossziget, *see* Sighetul Marmaţiei, p. 113			
Máriakút, *see* Rafajovce			
Mártonka, *see* Mala Martynka			
Maškivci, *see* Maškovce			
Maskócz, *see* Maškovce			
Maškovce [Sv] (Maškivci [Ru, U]; Maskócz [H]), since 1961 part of Vyšný Hrušov	Zemplén	Humenné	Slovakia

Village	Former Hungarian county or Galician district	Present administrative subdivision	Present country
**Nyžni Vorota [U] (Alsóvereczke [H]; Nyžni Verecky [Ru])	Bereg	Volovec'	Ukraine
Nyžnij Bystryj [U] (Alsóbistra [H]; Nyžnŷj Bŷstrŷj [Ru])	Máramaros	Chust	Ukraine
Nyžnij Komarnyk, *see* Nižný Komárnik			
Nyžnij Myrošiv, *see* Nižný Mirošov			
Nyžnij Orlyk, *see* Nižný Orlík			
Nyžnij Studenyj [U] (Alsóhidekpatak [H]; Nyžnŷj Studenŷj [Ru])	Máramaros	Mižhirja	Ukraine
Nyžnij Synevyr, *see* Synevyr			
Nyžnij Tvarožec/Tvarožec', *see* Nižný Tvarožec			
Nyžnij Verlych, *see* Nyžnij Orlyk			
Nyžnja Apša, *see* Dibrova, p. 112			
Nyžnja Hrabivnycja [U] (Alsógereben [H])	Bereg	Svaljava	Ukraine
Nyžnja Jablinka, *see* Nižná Jablonka			
Nyžnja Jadlova, *see* Nižná Jedl'ová			
Nyžnja Pysana, *see* Nižná Pisaná			
Nyžnja Radvan', *see* Nižná Radvaň			
Nyžnja Roztoka [U] (Alsóhatárszeg/ Nagyrosztoka [H]), now part of Roztoka, Bereg county			
Nyžnja Solotvyna [Ru, U] (Alsószlatina [H])	Ung	Užhorod	Ukraine
Nyžnja Vyznycja [U] (Alsóviznicze [H]; Nyžnja Vŷznycja [Ru])	Bereg	Mukačevo	Ukraine
Nyžnja Zbina, *see* Nižné Zbojné			
Nyžnje Bolotne [U] (Alsósárad [H]; Nyžnŷj Šard [Ru])	Ugocsa	Iršava	Ukraine
Nyžnje Selyšče [U] (Alsószelistye [H])	Máramaros	Chust	Ukraine
Nyžnje Zbijne, *see* Nižné Zbojne			
Nyžnji Čabynŷ, *see* Nižné Čabiny			
Nyžnji Slovinki, *see* Nižnie Slovinky			
Nyžnŷj Bŷstrŷj, *see* Nyžnij Bystryj			
Nyžnŷj Šard, *see* Nyžnje Bolotne			
Nyžnŷj Studenŷj, *see* Nyžnij Studenyj			
Óbajna, *see* Nižné Zbojné			
Obava [Ru, U] (Dunkófalva [H])	Bereg	Mukačevo	Ukraine
Obručné [Sv] (Abroncsos [H]; Obručne [Ru, U]; Obrucsnó [H])	Sáros	Stará L'ubovňa	Slovakia
Obrucsnó, *see* Obručné			
Ódavidháza, *see* Stare Davydkove			
Odrechova/Odrychova, *see* Odrzechowa			
Odrzechowa [P] (Odrechova [U]; Odrychova [Ru])	Sanok	Krosno	Poland
Ókemencze, *see* Kamjanycja			
Ökörmező, *see* Mižhirja			

Village	Former Hungarian county or Galician district	Present administrative subdivision	Present country
Ökröske, *see* Volica			
**Okružná [Sv] (Kereštvej [Ru]; Kiskőrósfő/Kőrösfő [H])	Sáros	Prešov	Slovakia
Ola, *see* Wola Michowa			
Oláhczertész, *see* Pidhirne			
Olajpatak, *see* Olejníkov			
Ol'chovec', *see* Olchowiec			
Olchowa [P] (Vilchova [Ru]; Vil'chova [U])	Lesko	Krosno	Poland
Olchowiec [P] (Ol'chovec'/ Vil'chivec' [U]; Vilchovec [Ru])	Krosno	Krosno	Poland
**Olejníkov [Sv] (Olajpatak/Olejnok [H]; Olijnyk [U])	Sáros	Prešov	Slovakia
Olejnok, *see* Olejníkov			
Oleksandrivka [U] (Ósándorfalva/ Sándorfalva [H]; Šandrovo [Ru])	Máramaros	Chust	Ukraine
Oleneve [U] (Olen'ovo [Ru]; Szarvaskút [H])	Bereg	Svaljava	Ukraine
Olen'ovo, *see* Oleneve			
Olešnyk [Ru, U] (Egres/Szőllősegres [H])	Ugocsa	Vynohradiv	Ukraine
Olijnyk, *see* Olejníkov			
Ol'ka [Ru, Sv, U] (Homonnaolyka/ Sztropkóolyka [H])	Zemplén	Humenné	Slovakia
Ol'šavica [Ru, Sv] (Nagyolsva [H]; Ol'šavycja [U])	Szepes	Spišská Nová Ves	Slovakia
Olšavka [Sv] (Kisolysó [H]; Ol'šavka [U]; Višavka [Ru])	Sáros	Svidník	Slovakia
Ol'šavycja, *see* Ol'šavica			
Ol'šinkov [Sv] (Meggyfalu [H]; Ol'šynkiv [U]; Vŷšŷnkiv [Ru])	Zemplén	Humenné	Slovakia
Ölyvös, *see* Vil'chivka			
Ondavafő, *see* Ondavka			
Ondavka [Ru, Sv, U] (Ondavafő [H])	Sáros	Bardejov	Slovakia
Onok [Ru, U] (Ilonokújfalu [H])	Ugocsa	Vynohradiv	Ukraine
Onokivci/Onokovci, *see* Onokivci, p. 113			
Oparivka, *see* Oparówka			
Oparówka [P] (Oparivka [U])	Krosno	Krosno	Poland
Ördögporuba, *see* Porúbka			
Ördögvágás, *see* Porúbka			
Őrhegyalja, *see* Pidhorjany			
Orichovycja [Ru, U] (Rahoncza [H])	Ung	Užhorod	Ukraine
Orjabina/Orjabyna, *see* Jarabina			
Orliv, *see* Orlov			
Orló, *see* Orlov			
Orlov [Sv] (Orliv [U]; Orló [H]; Virliv [Ru])	Sáros	Stará L'ubovňa	Slovakia
Ormód, *see* Brestiv			

Village	Former Hungarian county or Galician district	Present administrative subdivision	Present country
Uhlja [U] (Uglja [Ru]; Uglya [H])	Máramaros	Tjačiv	Ukraine
Uhryń [P] (Uhrin [Ru]; Uhryn [U])	Nowy Sącz	Nowy Sącz	Poland
Ujak/Uják, *see* Údol			
Újbajna, *see* Vyšné Zbojné			
Újbárd, *see* Nove Barovo			
Újdávidháza, *see* Nove Davydkove			
Újkemencze, *see* Novoselycja, Ung county			
Újrosztoka, *see* Nova Roztoka			
Újszék, *see* Nová Sedlica			
Újszemere, *see* Simerky			
Újszomolnok, *see* Smolník			
Uklyn [Ru, U] (Aklos [H])	Bereg	Svaljava	Ukraine
Ulič [Sv] (Ulics [H]; Ulyč [U]; Ulŷč [Ru]; Utczás [H])	Zemplén	Humenné	Slovakia
Ulics, *see* Ulič			
Ulicskriva, *see* Uličské Krivé			
Uličské Krivé [Sv] (Görbeszeg [H]; Kryvŷj [Ru]; Ulicskriva [H]; Ulyčs'ke-Kryve [U])	Zemplén	Humenné	Slovakia
Ulyč/Ulŷč, *see* Ulič			
Ulyčs'ke Kryve, *see* Uličské Krivé			
Ungbükkös, *see* Bukivceve			
Ungcsertész, *see* Čertiž			
Ungdarócz, *see* Dravci			
Unggesztenyés, *see* Linci			
Unghosszúmező, *see* Dovhe, Ung county			
Ungludás, *see* Husák			
Unglovasd, *see* Koňuš			
Ungordas, *see* Vovkove			
Ungpéteri, *see* Petrovce nad Laborcem			
Ungsasfalva, *see* Irljava			
Ungtölgyes, *see* Dibrivka, Ung county			
Ungvár, *see* Užhorod, p. 113			
Úrmező, *see* Rus'ke Pole			
Uście Gorlickie [P] (Uście Ruskie [P]; Uscja/Uscjo Ruskie [Ru]; Ustje Rus'ke [U])	Gorlice	Nowy Sącz	Poland
Uście/Uscja/Uscjo Ruskie, *see* Uście Gorlickie			
Uslavycja, *see* Osławica			
Ustje Rus'ke, *see* Uście Gorlickie			
Ustrzyki Górne [P] (Ustryky Horišni [U])	Lesko	Krosno	Poland
Ustryky Horišni, *see* Ustrzyki Górne			
Utczás, *see* Ulič			
Užhorod, *see* p. 113			
Užok [Ru, U] (Uzsok [H])	Ung	Velykyj Bereznyj	Ukraine
Uzsok, *see* Užok			

Village	Former Hungarian county or Galician district	Present administrative subdivision	Present country
Vabova, *see* Łabowa			
Vabovec, *see* Łabowiec			
Vadas, *see* Dyskovycja			
Vadászfalva, *see* Beňatina			
Vafka, *see* Wawrzka			
Vagrinec [Sv] (Felsővargony [H]; Vagrynec' [U])	Sáros	Svidník	Slovakia
Vagrynec', *see* Vagrinec			
Vajkvágása, *see* Valkovce			
Vajnág, *see* Vonihove			
Valaškovce [Sv] (Pásztorhegy [H]; Valaškuvci [Ru]; Valjaškivci [U])	Zemplén	Humenné	Slovakia
Valaškuvci, *see* Valaškovce			
Valea Vişeului [Ro] (Kismező [H]; Poljana [U]; Visóvölgy [H])	Máramaros	Maramureş	Romania
Valentovce [Sv], between 1880 and 1930 part of Zbudská Belá	Zemplén	Humenné	Slovakia
Valjaškivci, *see* Valaškovce			
Val'kiv, *see* Valkov			
Valkivci, *see* Valkovce			
Valkov [Sv] (Kisvalkó [H]; Val'kiv [Ru, U]) (since 1965 has ceased to exist)	Zemplén	Bardejov	Slovakia
Valkovce [Sv] (Vajkvágása [H]; Val'kivci [U]; Válykócz [H])	Sáros	Svidník	Slovakia
Válykócz, *see* Valkovce			
Vanivka, *see* Węglówka			
Vápeník [Sv] (Mészégető [H]; Vapenyk [U])	Sáros	Svidník	Slovakia
Vapenne, *see* Wapienne			
Vapenyk, *see* Vápeník			
Váradka [Sv] (Varadka [Ru, U])	Sáros	Bardejov	Slovakia
Váralja, *see* Pidhorod; Podhorod'			
Varechivci, *see* Varechovce			
Varechovce [Sv] (Varechivci [Ru, U]; Varehócz/Variháza [H])	Zemplén	Svidník	Slovakia
Varehócz, *see* Varechovce			
Variháza, *see* Varechovce			
Várkulcsa, *see* Ključarky			
Vavrinec [Ru, Sv] (Lőrinczvágása [H]; Vavrynec' [U])	Sáros	Vranov	Slovakia
Végardó, *see* Pidvynohradiv			
Végaszó, *see* Kolbasov			
Végcsarnó, *see* Krajné Čierno			
Végmártonka, *see* Krajnja Martynka			
Végortovány, *see* Krajná Porúbka			
Végpetri, *see* Petrová			
Végrosztoka, *see* Roztoky			

Village	Former Hungarian county or Galician district	Present administrative subdivision	Present country
Veléte, *see* Veljatyn			
Velikij Ruskov, *see* Vel'ký Ruskov			
Velikŷj Lipnik, *see* Vel'ký Lipník			
Veljatyn [Ru, U] (Veléte [H])	Ugocsa	Chust	Ukraine
Vel'ká Driečna [Sv] (Nagyderencs/ Sárosdricsna [H]; Velyka Drična [Ru, U], since 1960 part of Vladiča			
Vel'ká Pol'ana [Sv] (Nagypolány [H]; Velykŷ Poljanŷ [Ru]; Velyki Poljany [U]) (ceased to exist in 1980)	Zemplén	Humenné	Slovakia
Vel'ké Bukovce [Sv] (Nagybukócz/ Sárosbukócz [H]; Velykŷj Bukovec [Ru]; Velykyi Bukovec' [U]), since 1964 part of Bukovce			
Vel'ké Staškovce [Sv] (Nagytavas/ Sárossztaskócz [H]; Velyki Staškivci [U]; Velykŷ Staškivci [Ru]), part of Staškovce			
Velkő, *see* Vel'krop			
Vel'krop [Sv] (Bekrip [Ru]; Velkő [H]; Vel'krip [U])	Zemplén	Svidník	Slovakia
Vel'ký Lipník [Sv] (Nagyhársas/ Nagylipnik [H]; Velikŷj Lipnik [Ru]; Velykyj Lypnyk [U])	Szepes	Stará L'ubovňa	Slovakia
**Vel'ký Ruskov [Sv] (Nagyruszka [H]; Velikij Ruskov [Ru]), since 1964 part of Nový Ruskov	Zemplén	Trebišov	Slovakia
Vel'ký Sulín [Sv] (Nagyszulin [H]; Vel'kŷj Sulin [Ru]; Velykyj Sulyn [U]), since 1961 part of Sulín			
Vel'kŷj Sulin, *see* Vel'ký Sulín			
Velšnja, *see* Wilsznia			
Velyka Čengava/Velyka Čynhava, *see* Boržavs'ke			
Velyka Drična, *see* Vel'ka Driečna			
Velyka Kopanja [Ru, U] (Felsőveresmart [H])	Ugocsa	Vynohradiv	Ukraine
Velyka Poljana, *see* Vel'ká Pol'ana			
Velyka Roztoka [U] (Beregrosztoka/ Gázló [H]; Roztoka [Ru])	Bereg	Iršava	Ukraine
Velyka Turycja, *see* Turycja			
Velykopole, *see* Wielopole			
Velyki Komjaty [U] (Komját/Magyar- komját [H]; Velyki Komnjata [Ru])	Ugocsa	Vynohradiv	Ukraine
Velyki Lazy [U] (Nagyláz [H]; Velyki Lazŷ [Ru])	Ung	Užhorod	Ukraine
Velyki Lučky [Ru, U] (Nagylucska [H])	Bereg	Mukačevo	Ukraine

Village	Former Hungarian county or Galician district	Present administrative subdivision	Present country
Velyki Staškivci, *see* Vel'ke Staškovce			
Velykŷ Poljanŷ/Velyky Poljany, *see* Vel'ka Pol'ana			
Velykŷ Staškivci, *see* Vel'ke Staškovce			
Velykyj Bereznyj, *see* p. 113			
Velykyj Bočkov, *see* Velykyj Byčkiv			
Velykyj Byčkiv [U] (Nagybocskó [H]; Velykyj Bočkov [Ru])	Máramaros	Rachiv	Ukraine
Velykyj Lypnyk, *see* Vel'ký Lipník			
Velykyj Rakovec' [Ru, U] (Nagyrákócz [H])	Ugocsa	Iršava	Ukraine
Velykyj Sulyn, *see* Vel'ký Sulín			
Vendági, *see* Hostovice			
Venecia [Sv] (Venecija [U]; Venécze [H]), since 1943 part of Lukov			
Venécze, *see* Venecia			
Verbas, *see* Stari Vrbas, p. 113			
Verbjaž [Ru, U] (Verebes [H])	Bereg	Volovec'	Ukraine
*Verchni Remety [U] (Felsőremete [H]; Vŷšni Remeta [Ru])	Bereg	Berehovo	Ukraine
Verchni Verec'ky, *see* Verchni Vorota			
Verchni Vorota [U] (Felsővereczke [H]; Verchni Verecky [U]; Vŷšni Verecky [Ru])	Bereg	Volovec'	Ukraine
Verchnij Bystryj [U] (Vŷšnyj Bŷstrŷj [Ru]), part of Majdan, Máramaros county			
Verchnij Koroslov, *see* Hreblja			
Verchnij Studenyj [U] (Felsőhidegpatak [H]; Vŷšnŷj Studenŷj [Ru])	Máramaros	Mižhirja	Ukraine
Verchnja Apša, *see* Verchnje Vodjane			
Verchnja Hrabivnycja [U] (Felső-gereben [H]; Vŷšnja Hrabovnycja [Ru])	Bereg	Volovec'	Ukraine
Verchnja Solotvyna [U] (Felsőszlatina [H]; Vŷšnja Solotvyna [Ru])	Ung	Užhorod	Ukraine
Verchnja Vyznycja [U] (Felsőviznicze [H]; Vŷšnja Vŷznycja [Ru])	Bereg	Mukačevo	Ukraine
Verchnje Vodjane [U] (Felsőapsa [H]; Verchnja Apša [U]; Vŷšnja Apša [Ru])	Máramaros	Rachiv	Ukraine
Verchovnja, *see* Wierchomla			
Verchovyna-Bystra [U] (Bŷstrŷj [Ru]; Határszög [H])	Ung	Velykyj Bereznyj	Ukraine
Verebes, *see* Verbjaž			
Verécze, *see* Verjacja			
Veremin', *see* Weremień			
Vereshegy, *see* Poráč			
Verjacja [Ru, U] (Verécze [H])	Ugocsa	Vynohradiv	Ukraine
Verymin, *see* Weremień			
Vetlyna, *see* Wetlina			
Vezérszállás, *see* Pidpolozzja			

Village	Former Hungarian county or Galician district	Present administrative subdivision	Present country
Vŷšnja Vilšava, *see* Vyšná Ol'šava			
Vyšnja Vladyča, *see* Vyšná Vladiča			
Vŷšnja Vŷznycja, *see* Verchnja Vyznycja			
Vŷšnja Zbina, *see* Vyšné Zbojné			
Vyšnje Zbijne, *see* Vyšné Zbojne			
Vŷšnji Slovinki, *see* Vyšnie Slovinky			
**Vyšný Hrabovec [Sv] (Kisgyertyános/ Oroszhrabócz/Sztropkóhrabócz [H]; Vŷšnij Hrabovec [Ru]; Vyšnij Hrabovec' [U]), since 1961 part of Turany nad Ondavou	Sáros	Svidník	Slovakia
Vyšný Komárnik [Sv] (Felsőkomárnok [H]; Vŷšnij Komarnyk [Ru]; Vyšnij Komarnyk [U])	Sáros	Svidník	Slovakia
Vyšný Mirošov [Sv] (Vŷšnij Myrošiv [Ru]; Vyšnij Myrošiv [U])	Sáros	Svidník	Slovakia
Vyšný Orlík [Sv] (Felsőodor/Felsőorlich [H]; Vyšnij Orlyk [U]; Vŷšnij Verlych [Ru])	Sáros	Svidník	Slovakia
Vyšný Tvarožec [Sv] (Felsőtarócz [H]; Vŷšnij Tvarožec [Ru]; Vyšnij Tvarožec' [U])	Sáros	Bardejov	Slovakia
Vŷšnyj Bŷstrŷj, *see* Verchnij Bystryj			
Vŷšnŷj Šard, *see* Šyroke			
Vŷšnŷj Studenŷj, *see* Verchnij Studenyj			
Vyšnŷj Synŷvyr, *see* Synevyrs'ka Poljana			
Vysočany, *see* Wysoczany			
Vysova, *see* Wysowa			
Vŷšovatka, *see* Wyszowadka			
Vŷšovo, *see* Vişeul de Sus, p. 113			
Vŷšŷnkiv, *see* Ol'šinkiv			
Wapienne [P] (Vapenne [Ru, U])	Gorlice	Nowy Sącz	Poland
Wawrzka [P] (Vafka [Ru, U])	Grybów	Nowy Sącz	Poland
Węglówka [P] (Vanivka [U])	Krosno	Krosno	Poland
Weremień [P] (Veremin' [U]; Verymin [Ru])	Lesko	Krosno	Poland
Wetlina [P] (Vetlyna [Ru, U])	Lesko	Krosno	Poland
Wielopole [P] (Velykopole [Ru, U])	Sanok	Krosno	Poland
Wierchomla [P] (Verchovnja/Virchovnja [Ru]; Virchovnja Velyka [U]; Wierchomla Wielka [P])	Nowy Sącz	Nowy Sącz	Poland
Wierchomla Mała [P] (Virchimka [Ru]; Virchivka Mala [U])	Nowy Sącz	Nowy Sącz	Poland
Wierchomla Wielka, *see* Wierchomla			
Wilsznia [P] (Velšnja/Vilšnja [Ru]; Vil'šnja [U]) (ceased to exist after 1947)	Krosno	Krosno	Poland

Village	Former Hungarian county or Galician district	Present administrative subdivision	Present country
Wirchne [P] (Virchnja [Ru, U]) (ceased to exist after 1947)	Gorlice	Nowy Sącz	Poland
Wisłoczek [P] (Vysločok [U])	Sanok	Krosno	Poland
Wisłok Dolny [P] (Vyslik Nŷžnŷj [Ru]; Vyslok Nyžnyj [U]) (ceased to exist after 1947)	Sanok	Krosno	Poland
Wisłok Gorny [P] (Vyslik Vŷžnŷj [Ru]; Vyslok Horišnyj [U])	Sanok	Krosno	Poland
Wisłok Wielki [P] (Vyslik Velykŷj [Ru]; Vyslok Velykyj [U])	Sanok	Krosno	Poland
Wojkowa [P] (Vikova [Ru, U]; Vojkova [U])	Nowy Sącz	Nowy Sącz	Poland
Wola Cieklińska [P] (Vola Ceklynska [Ru]; Volja Ceklyns'ka [U])	Jasło	Krosno	Poland
Wola Górzańska [P] (Volja Horjans'ka [U])	Lesko	Krosno	Poland
Wola Matiaszowa [P] (Bereščajska Vola [Ru]; Vola Matijošova [U])	Lesko	Krosno	Poland
Wola Michowa [P] (Ola/Vola Michova [Ru]; Volja Myhova [U])	Lesko	Krosno	Poland
Wola Niżna [P] (Vola Nŷznja [Ru]; Volja Nyžnja [U])	Sanok	Krosno	Poland
Wola Piotrowa [P] (Vola Petrova [Ru]; Petrova Volja [U])	Sanok	Krosno	Poland
Wola Sękowa [P] (Vola Synkova [Ru]; Sen'kova Volja [U])	Sanok	Krosno	Poland
Wola Wyżna [P] (Vola Vŷšnja [Ru]; Volja Vyžnja [U]) (ceased to exist after 1947)	Sanok	Krosno	Poland
Wolica [P] (Volyca [Ru]; Volycja [U])	Sanok	Krosno	Poland
Wólka [P] (Vilka [Ru]; Vil'ka [U]; Wulka [P]) (ceased to exist after 1947)	Sanok	Krosno	Poland
Wołkowyja [P] (Volkovŷja [Ru]; Vovkovŷja [U]; Vukovŷja [Ru])	Lesko	Krosno	Poland
Wołosate [P] (Volosate [U])	Lesko	Krosno	Poland
Wołowiec [P] (Volovec [Ru]; Volovec' [U])	Gorlice	Nowy Sącz	Poland
Wołtuszowa [P] (Voltušova [U])	Sanok	Krosno	Poland
Wróblik Królewski [P] (Vorobik [Ru]; Voroblyk Korolivs'kyj [U])	Krosno	Krosno	Poland
Wróblik Szlachecki [P] (Vorobik [Ru]; Voroblyk Šljachets'kyj [U])	Sanok	Krosno	Poland
Wulka, see Wólka			
Wysoczany [P] (Vysočany [Ru, U])	Sanok	Krosno	Poland
Wysowa [P] (Vysova [Ru, U])	Gorlice	Nowy Sącz	Poland
Wyszowadka [P] (Vyševatka [U]; Vŷsovatka [Ru])	Jasło	Krosno	Poland
Zabłotce [P] (Zabolotci [U])	Sanok	Krosno	Poland
Zabolotci, see Zabłotce			
Zabrid' [U] (Révhely [H]; Zabrod' [Ru])	Ung	Velykyj Bereznyj	Ukraine

Village	Former Hungarian county or Galician district	Present administrative subdivision	Present country
Zabrod', *see* Zabrid'			
Zabrodja, *see* Zabrodzie			
Zabrodzie [P] (Zabrodja [U])	Lesko	Krosno	Poland
Zadils'kyj [Ru, U] (Rekesz [H])	Bereg	Volovec'	Ukraine
Zadno'je, *see* Pryboržavs'ke			
Zahatja, *see* Zahattja			
Zahattja [U] (Hátmeg [H]; Zahatja [Ru])	Bereg	Iršava	Ukraine
Zahočevja, *see* Zahoczewie			
Zahoczewie [P] (Zahočevja [U]; Zalačyvja [Ru])	Lesko	Krosno	Poland
Zahorb [Ru, U] (Határhegy [H])	Ung	Velkyj Bereznyj	Ukraine
Zahutyń [P] (Zahutyn' [Ru, U])	Sanok	Krosno	Poland
Zajgó, *see* Dusyna			
Zalačyvja, *see* Zahoczewie			
Zaluž, *see* Zalužžja			
Zalužžja [U] (Beregkisalmás/Kisalmás [H]; Zaluž [Ru])	Bereg	Mukačevo	Ukraine
Zandranova, *see* Zyndranova			
Zariča, Ugocsa county, *see* Zaričča			
Zariča, Ung county, *see* Zaričeve			
Zaričča [U] (Alsókaraszló [H]; Zariča [Ru])	Ugocsa	Iršava	Ukraine
Zaričeve [U] (Drugetháza [H]; Zariča [Ru])	Ung	Perečyn	Ukraine
Zárnya, *see* Pryboržavs'ke			
Zaslav, *see* Zasław			
Zaslavje, *see* Zasław			
Zasław [P] (Zaslav [Ru]; Zaslavje [U]; Zasławie [P])	Sanok	Krosno	Poland
Žatkivci, *see* Žatkovce			
Žatkovce [Sv] (Žatkivci [Ru, U]; Zsetek [H])	Sáros	Prešov	Slovakia
Zatvarnycja, *see* Zatwarnica			
Zatwarnica [P] (Zatvarnycja [U])	Lesko	Krosno	Poland
Závada [Sv] (Hegyzávod [H]; Zavada [Ru, U]	Zemplén	Vranov	Slovakia
Zavadka [Ru, U] (Rákócziszállás [H])	Bereg	Volovec'	Ukraine
Zavadka, Sanok district, *see* Morochownica			
*Závadka [Sv] (Csergőzávod [H]; Zavadka [Ru, U])	Sáros	Prešov	Slovakia
Závadka [Sv] (Görögfalu [H]; Zavadka [Ru, U])	Szepes	Spišská Nová Ves	Slovakia
Zavadka [U] (Kiscsongova [H]; Mala Čengava [Ru])	Ugocsa	Vynohradiv	Ukraine
Zavadka Morochivs'ka, *see* Morochownica			
Zavadka Rymanivs'ka, *see* Zawadka Rymanowska			
Zavatka, *see* Zawadka Rymanowska			
Zaviddja, *see* Závodie			
Zavij, *see* Zawój			
Zaviz, *see* Zawóz			

Village	Former Hungarian county or Galician district	Present administrative subdivision	Present country
Závodie [Sv] (Zaviddja [U]; Zavŷdja [Ru]), since 1961 part of Sulín			
Zavoj/Zavoji, *see* Zawoje			
Zavosyna, *see* Zavosyne			
Zavosyne [U] (Szénástelek [H]; Zavosyna [Ru])	Ung	Velykyj Bereznyj	Ukraine
Zavŷdja, *see* Závodie			
Zavydove [U] (Dávidfalva [H]; Zavydovo [Ru])	Bereg	Mukačevo	Ukraine
Zavydovo, *see* Zavydove			
Zawadka Morochowska, *see* Morochownica			
Zawadka Rymanowska [P] (Zavadka Rymanivs'ka [U]; Zavatka [Ru])	Sanok	Krosno	Poland
Zawój [P] (Zavíj [U]) (ceased to exist after 1947)	Lesko	Krosno	Poland
Zawoje [P] (Zavoj [Ru]; Zavoji [Ru, U]) (ceased to exist after 1947)	Sanok	Krosno	Poland
Zawóz [P] (Zaviz [U])	Lesko	Krosno	Poland
Zbij, *see* Zboj			
Zbijne, *see* Zbojné			
Zboiska [P, Ru] (Zbojis'ka [U])	Sanok	Krosno	Poland
Zboj [Sv] (Harczos [H]; Zbij [U]; Zbuj [Ru])	Zemplén	Humenné	Slovakia
Zbojis'ka, *see* Zboiska			
Zbojné [Sv] (Zbijne [U])	Zemplén	Humenné	Slovakia
Žborivci [U] (Rónafalu [H]; Žborovci [Ru])	Bereg	Mukačevo	Ukraine
Zbudská Belá [Sv] (Izbugyabéla [H]; Zbuds'ka Bila [Ru, U])	Zemplén	Humenné	Slovakia
Zbudský Rokytov [Sv] (Izbugyarokitó [H]; Zbuds'kyj Rokytiv [U]), since 1970 part of Rokytov pri Humennom			
Zbuj, *see* Zboj			
Zbyny [U] (Izbonya [H]; Zbŷnŷ [Ru])	Bereg	Volovec'	Ukraine
Ždeneve [U] (Szarvasháza [H]; Ždjen'ovo [Ru])	Bereg	Volovec'	Ukraine
Ždjen'ovo, *see* Ždeneve			
Zdvyžen', *see* Zwierzyń			
Żdynia [P] (Ždynja [Ru, U])	Gorlice	Nowy Sącz	Poland
Žegestiv, *see* Żegiestów			
Żegiestów [P] (Žegestiv [Ru, U])	Nowy Sącz	Nowy Sącz	Poland
Zelló, *see* Zvalá			
Zemplénbukócz, *see* Malé Bukovce			
Zempléndricsna, *see* Mala Driečna			
Zemplénoroszi, *see* Ruské			
Zemplénszomolnok, *see* Smolník			
Zemplénsztaskócz, *see* Malé Staškovce			

Village	Former Hungarian county or Galician district	Present administrative subdivision	Present country
Żerdenka [P] (Žerdenka [U]; Žerdynka [Ru])	Lesko	Krosno	Poland
Żernica Niżna [P] (Žernycja [Ru]; Žernycja Nyžnja [U]) (after 1947 ceased to exist)	Lesko	Krosno	Poland
Żernica Wyżna [P] (Žernycja Vyžnja [U]) (after 1945 ceased to exist)	Lesko	Krosno	Poland
Žernycja Nyžnja, *see* Żernica Niżna			
Žernycja/Žernycja Vyžnja, *see* Żernica Wyżna			
Zloc'ke, *see* Złockie			
Złockie [P] (Zloc'ke [U]; Zlockie [Ru])	Nowy Sącz	Nowy Sącz	Poland
Znjaceve [U] (Ignécz [H]; Znjac'ovo [Ru])	Bereg	Mukačevo	Ukraine
Znjac'ovo, *see* Znjaceve			
Zolotareve [U] (Ötvösfalva [H]; Zolotarjovo [Ru])	Máramaros	Chust	Ukraine
Zolotarjovo, *see* Zolotareve			
Zsetek, *see* Žatkovce			
Zsilip, *see* Plavja			
Zsukó, *see* Žukove			
Zubeńsko [P] (Zubens'ko [U]) (ceased to exist after 1947)	Lesko	Krosno	Poland
Zubné [Sv] (Tölgyeshegy [H]; Zubnyj [U]; Zubnŷj [Ru])	Zemplén	Humenné	Slovakia
Zubnyj/Zubnŷj, *see* Zubné			
Zubrače, *see* Żubracze			
Żubracze [P] (Zubrače [U]; Zubrjači [Ru])	Lesko	Krosno	Poland
Zubrik, *see* Zubrzyk			
Zubrjači, *see* Żubracze			
Zubryk, *see* Zubrzyk			
Zubrzyk [P] (Zubrik [Ru]; Zubryk [U])	Nowy Sącz	Nowy Sącz	Poland
Zuella, *see* Zvala			
Zúgó, *see* Huklyvyj			
Zuhatag, *see* Stakčianska Roztoka			
Žukove [U] (Zsukó [H]; Žukovo [Ru])	Bereg	Mukačevo	Ukraine
Žukovo, *see* Žukove			
Žurdziv, *see* Dziurdziów			
Zvala [Ru, Sv, U] (Zelló/Zuella [H]) (ceased to exist in 1980)	Zemplén	Humenné	Slovakia
Zwierzyń [P] (Zdvyžen' [U])	Lesko	Krosno	Poland
Žydivs'ke/Žydivske, *see* Żydowskie			
Żydowskie [P] (Žydivs'ke [U]; Žydivskie/Žydivskŷj [Ru])	Jasło	Krosno	Poland
Žydivskŷj, *see* Żydowskie			
Zyndranova, *see* Zyndranowa			
Zyndranowa [P] (Dzyndranova/Zandranova [Ru]; Zyndranova [Ru, U])	Krosno	Krosno	Poland

For Further Reading

A. Bibliographical Guides

The works listed below in sections B and C deal primarily or exclusively with Carpatho-Rusyn life in the United States. The only other separately published bibliography on the subject is a brief annotated listing in Paul R. Magocsi, *Carpatho-Ruthenians in North America*, The Balch Institute Historical Reading Lists, No. 31 (Philadelphia, Pa., 1976). More recent literature is found in Paul Robert Magocsi, *Carpatho-Rusyn Studies: An Annotated Bibliography*, Vol. I: *1975-1984* (New York and London: Garland Publishing, 1988). As for materials in libraries and other resource centers, see Edward Kasinec, *The Carpatho-Ruthenian Immigration in the United States: A Preliminary Note on Sources in Some United States Repositories*, Harvard Ukrainian Research Institute Offprint Series, No. 6 (Cambridge, Mass., 1975). There is also a useful survey of documentary sources about emigration in Subcarpathian (Transcarpathian) archives in: H.V. Bozhuk and V.V. Pal'ok, "Dokumenty Zakarpats'koho oblasnoho derzhavnoho arkhivu pro trudovu emihratsiiu zakarpattsiv u SShA ta Kanadu," in D.M. Fedaka, ed., *Ukraïns'ki Karpaty* (Uzhhorod: Karpaty, 1993), pp.77-86.

The basic source for the study of Carpatho-Rusyns in America are the more than 60 newspapers, journals, and annual almanacs published by various religious and secular organizations, which contain a wide variety of news reports, biographies of immigrant leaders, statistical data on organizations, and other valuable materials. Most of these serials have been preserved on microfilm and are listed in Frank Renkiewicz, *The Carpatho-Ruthenian Microfilm Project: A Guide to Newspapers and Periodicals* (St. Paul, Minn.: University of Minnesota Immigration History Research Center, 1979). An annotated bibliographical index to the oldest and most important Rusyn-American newspaper has been undertaken: James M. Evans, *Guide to the Amerikansky Russky Viestnik*, Vol. I: *1894-1914* (Fairview, N. J.: Carpatho-Rusyn Research Center, 1979). There is also much information to be found in individual parish memorial books and histories issued by a large number of churches.

As for material on the European homeland, there are several bibliographies. See, for instance, three works by Paul Robert Magocsi: "An Historiographical Guide to Subcarpathian Rus'," *Austrian History Yearbook*, IX-X (Houston, Texas, 1973-74), pp. 201-265; *The Shaping of a National Identity: Subcarpathian Rus', 1848-1948* (Cambridge, Mass. and London, England: Harvard University Press, 1978), esp. pp. 465-585; *The Rusyns of Slovakia: An Historical Survey* (New York: East European Quarterly/Columbia University Press, 1993) pp. 141-170; and Tadeusz Zagórzański, *Łemkowie i Łemkowszczyzna: Materiały do bibliografii* (Warsaw: Studenckie Koło Przewodników Beskidzkich, 1984).

B. Documentary Sources

Although many of the items in this section deal with developments in Europe, they are nonetheless listed here because they were published by Carpatho-Rusyns in the United States or Canada, and therefore they reflect the political views held by the group at various times.

American Carpathian-Russian Congress. *Protest to Honorable James F. Byrnes, Secretary, U. S. State Department, Peace Conference, Paris France (Europe). Re: Annexation of Podkarpatska Rus' (Ruthenia) to Soviet Union*. Munhall, Pa., 1946.

Carpatho-Russia, Clue to Soviet Policy?. Foreign Nationality Groups in the United States, No. 154. Washington, D.C.: Office of Strategic Services, Foreign Nationalities Branch, 11 October 1943.

Chornak, Orestes. *Documentae Appellationis*. Bridgeport, September 20, 1931.

Declaration and Memorandum of the Russian Council of Carpatho-Russia in Lwow, of the League for the Liberation of Carpatho-Russia in America, and of the League for the Liberation of Carpatho-Russia in Canada. n.p., 1919.

Fentsik, Stepan A. *Uzhgorod-Amerika: putevyia zamietki, 13.X. 1934-19.V.1935*. Uzhhorod: Nash put', 1935.

[Gerovskij, Aleksij]. *Karpatskaja Rus' v česskom jarmi*. n.p., 1939.

Jaka majet byti konstitucija Podkarpatskoj Rusi. Homestead, Pa.: Rusin Information Bureau, 192?

Karpatorossy v Amerike, ostavte hlubokij son: programa, resolucii Amerikanskoho Karpatorusskoho Jedinstva. Gary, Ind.: Amerikanskoje Karpatorusskoje Jedinstvo, [1941].

Karpatskij, Ivan. *Piznajte pravdu*. New York: Komitet oborony Karpatskoji Ukrajiny, 1939.

Krizis konstitucii i nikoli gubernatora Podkarpatskoj Rusi. Homestaed, Pa.: Rusin Information Bureau, 192?

Lemko Relief Committee in the U.S.A. Trumbull, Conn., 1962.

Lukach, Mykhayl; Lukach, Elena; Baran, Anna; Volchak, Mykhalyna. *Pravda o ridnim kraiu 1963: s podorozhy 2-i delegatsyy Obshchestva karpatorusskykh kanadtsev do ChSSR, PNR y SSSR*. Toronto: Tsentral'nyi komytet Ob shchestva karpatorusskykh kanadtsev, 1964.

A Memorandum in Behalf of Podkarpatskaja Rus' (Sub-Carpatho Rus') to the State Department of the United States of America and Representatives of the United States of America at the World Security Conference. Munhall, Pa., 1945.

Memorandum of the Carpatho-Russian Council in America Concerning Eastern Galicia with Lemkowschina and Bukovina. New York, 1921.

Memorandum Russkago kongressa v Amerikie, sozvannago 'Soiuzom osvobozhdeniia Prikarpatskoi Rusi', posviashchaemyi svobodnomu russkomu narodu v Rossii, Russkomu uchreditel'nomu sobraniu, Russkomu pravitel'stvu. n.p., [1917].

Michaylo, George. *A Memorandum in Behalf of Podkarpatskaja Rus to the State Department of the United States of America and Representatives of the U.S.A. at the World Security Conference*. Munhall, Pa., April 23, 1945.

0 chîm radyly na Vsenarodnom vîchu d. 26 novembra 1903 v Yonkers, N.I. Scranton, Pa.: Amerykanskii russkii narodnyi fond, 1904.

Protest. Pittsburgh: Greek Catholic Diocese, 1945.

Protokol zapysnytsa zasîdaniia Narodnoho kongressa amerykanskykh rusynov pod okranoiu y rukovodstvom Amerykanskoi Narodnoi Radŷ Uhro-Rusynov poderzhannoho v Homsted, Pa., dnia 15, 16 sent. 1919-ho roka. Homestead, Pa., 1919.

Slivka, John, ed. *Historical Mirror: Sources of the Rusin and Hungarian Greek Rite Catholics in the United States of America, 1884-1963*. Brooklyn, N.Y., 1978.

Slovensko-podkarpatsko-ruska hranica. Homestead, Pa.: Rusin Information Bureau, 192?.

Statut Tovarystva "Rus'ko-amerykan'skoy Radŷ" v Spoluchenŷkh Derzhavakh Pôvn. Ameryky. Philadelphia, Pa., 1914.

Statuty Karpato-Russkoj Greko Kaftoličeskoj Jeparchii Voštočnaho Obrjada Cerkvi v Sojedinennych Štatach Ameriki/By-Laws of the Carpatho-Russian Greek Catholic Diocese of the Eastern Rite Church in the United States of America. n.p., n.d.

Takach, Basil. *Ot episkopa amerikanskich greko-katoličeskich rusinov*. Homestead, Pa., 1931.

Toth, Alexis. *Letters, Articles, Papers, and Sermons*, 4 vols. Edited and translated by George Soldatow. Chilliwack, British Columbia: Synaxis Press and Minneapolis, Minn.: AARDM Press, 1978-88.

Tretii vseobschchii Karpatorusskii kongress v Amerikie, sostoiavshiisia v N'iu-Iorkie s 28-31 dekabria 1919 g. i 1-go ianvaria 1920 goda. New York: Karpatorusskaia narodnaia organizatsiia v Amerikie, 1920.

Ustav Obshchestva Karpatorusskikh Kanadtsev/ Constitution of the Society of Carpatho-Russian Canadians [Toronto, 1961].

Yuhasz, Michael. *Petition Concerning the Educational Complaints of the Autonomous Carpatho-Russian Territory South of the Carpathian Mountains . . . Presented to the League of Nations*. Homestead, Pa.: Amerikansky russky viestnik, 1932.

————. *Wilson's Principles in Czechoslovak Practice: The Situation of the Carpatho-Russian People Under the Czech Yoke*. Homestead, Pa.: Amerikansky russky viestnik, 1929.

Žatkovič, Gregory I. *Otkrytie-Exposé byvšeho gubernatora Podkarpatskoj Rusi, o Podkarpatskoj Rusi*. 2nd ed. Homestead, Pa.: Rusin Information Bureau, 1921.

————. *Spravoizdanije Predsidatel'a Direktoriuma Avtonomičnoj Rusinii, na Pervyj Narodnyj Kongress*. Homestead, Pa.: Amerikansky russky viestnik, 1919.

————. *The Rusin Question in a Nutshell*. n.p., 1923.

Zeedick, Peter Ivan and Smor, Adalbert Michael. *Naše stanovišče otnositel'no aktual'nych voprosov Amerikanskoj Gr. Kaftoličeskoj Russkoj Cerkvi Vostočnoho Obrjada*. Homestead, Pa.: Literaturnyj Komitet Sojedinenija Gr. Kaft. Russkich Bratstv, 1934.

C. Secondary Sources

American Carpatho-Russian Orthodox Greek Catholic Diocese Commemorative Jubilee Journal: Fiftieth Golden Anniversary, 1938-1988. Johnstown, Pa.: American Carpatho-Russian Orthodox Greek Catholic Diocese, 1988.

American Carpatho-Russian Orthodox Greek Catholic Diocese of U.S.A. Silver Anniversary 1938-1963. Johnstown, Pa., 1963.

Andrukhovych, K. *Z zhyttia rusyniv v Amerytsi: spomyn z rokiv 1889-1892*. Kolomyia, 1904.

Bachyns'kyi, Iuliian. *Ukraïns'ka immigratsiia v Z"iedynenykh Derzhavakh Ameryky*. L'viv, 1914.

Baran, Alexander. "Carpatho-Ukrainian Emigration, 1870-1914." In Jaroslav Rozumnyj, ed. *New Soil—Old Roots: The Ukrainian Experience in Canada*. Winnipeg: Ukrainian Academy of Arts and Sciences in Canada, 1983, pp. 252-275.

Barriger, Lawrence. *Good Victory: Metropolitan Orestes Chornock and the American Carpatho-Russian Orthodox Greek Catholic Diocese*. Brookline, Mass.: Holy Cross Orthodox Press, 1985.

Bensin, Basil M. *History of the Russian Orthodox Greek Catholic Church of North America*. New York, 1941.

Berezhnyi, Petro; Bek, Petro; Hiba, Mykhailo. *V im"ia pravdy: do uvahy lemkam, prozhyvaiuchym v Amerytsi.* New York, 1962.

Bidwell, Charles E. *The Language of Carpatho-Ruthenian Publications in America.* Pittsburgh, Pa.: University of Pittsburgh Center for International Studies, 1971.

Blaško, Štefan. *Miriam Teresa, Faithful in a Little: Demjanovich Roots.* Toronto: Maria Magazine, 1984.

Boruch, Ivan Gr. *Hospodarka ukraynoradykal'nŷkh popov v 'Soiuzî'.* New York, 1903.

————. *Nashe tserkovno-narodnoe dielo v Amerikie ot nachala nashei emigratsii do nynieshnikh dnei.* New York, 1950.

Brinda, Mikhail. "Bekheroviane v Kanadi." In *Karpatorusskii kalendar Lemko-Soiuza na 1945.* Yonkers, N.Y., 1944, pp. 100-102.

Byzantine Slavonic Rite Catholic Diocese of Pittsburgh Silver Jubilee 1924-1949. McKeesport, Pa.: Prosvita, 1949.

Čapek, T. "Podkarpatští rusíni v Americe před valkou a za valky," *Naše revoluce,* IV (Prague, 1926), pp. 267-279.

Chambre, Renee, *Sister Miriam Teresa: Apostle of Unity.* Mahwah, N.J.: Unity League, 1970.

Conklin, Margaret M. *An American Teresa,* 2nd ed., Patterson, N.J.: Charles J. Demjanovich, 1946.

Dančak, František. "Z galéria našich rodol'ubov: Emil Kubek." In *Gréckokatolický kalendár 1977.* Bratislava, 1976, pp. 151-155.

Danko, Joseph. "Plebiscite of Carpatho-Ruthenians in the United States Recommending Union of Carpatho-Ruthenia with Czechoslovakia," *Annals of the Ukrainian Academy of Arts and Sciences in the United States,* XI, 1-2 (New York, 1964), pp. 184-207.

————. "Rol' zakarpats'koï emihratsiï v SShA u vyrishenni doli Zakarpattia v 1918-1919 rokakh." In D. M. Fedaka, ed. *Ukraïns'ki Karpaty.* Uzhhorod: Karpaty, 1993, pp. 169-183.

Davis, Jerome. *The Russians and Ruthenians in America: Bolsheviks or Brothers?* New York: George H. Doran, 1922.

Dorko, Nicholas. "The Geographical Background of the Faithful of the Apostolic Exarchate of Pittsburgh," *Slovak Studies,* IV (Cleveland and Rome, 1964), pp. 217-226.

Duly, William. *The Rusyns of Minnesota.* Minneapolis, Minn.: Rusin Association of Minnesota, 1993.

Dushnyk, Walter. "Ukrainians and Ruthenians." In Joseph S. Roucek and Bernard Eisenberg, eds. *America's Ethnic Politics.* Westport, Conn. and London, England: Greenwood Press, 1982, pp. 367-385.

"[Dvadtsiat'] 20-litye Lemko-Soiuza v Ameryki." In Symeon S. Pŷzh, ed. *Iubyleinŷi karpatorusskyi kalendar' Lemko-Soiuza na hod 1951.* Yonkers, N.Y., 1950, pp. 23-59.

Dyrud, Keith P. "East Slavs: Rusins, Ukrainians, Russians, and Belorussians." In June Drenning Holmquist, ed. *They Chose Minnesota: A Survey of the State's Ethnic Groups.* St. Paul, Minn.: Minnesota Historical Society, 1981, pp. 405-422.

————. *The Quest for the Rusyn Soul: The Politics of Religion and Culture in Eastern Europe and America, 1890-World War I.* Philadelphia, London, and Toronto: Associated University Preses for the Balch Institute Press, 1992.

Dzwonczyk, J. H., ed. *Iubileinyi al'manakh, 1900-1940, Obshchestva russkikh bratstv v S.Sh.A.* Philadelphia: Pravda, 1939.

[Fiftieth] 50th Anniversary Almanac of the Lemko Association of USA and Canada/Iubyleinŷi al'manakh 50-lityia Lemko Soiuza v SShA y Kanadi. [Yonkers, N.Y.: Lemko Soiuz, 1979].

First Pontifical Divine Liturgy and Solemn Installation of His Excellency, Most Reverend Orestes P. Chornock of the Carpatho-Russian Greek Catholic Diocese of the Eastern Rite in the United States. Bridgeport, Conn., 1938.

Fischer, Stanisław. "Wyjazdy Łemków nadosławskich na roboty zarobkowe do Ameryki," *Materiały Muzeum Budownictwa Ludowego w Sanoku,* No. 6 (Sanok, 1967), pp. 7-8.

Goman, John D. *Galician-Rusins on the Iron Range.* Minneapolis, Minn.: p.a., 1990.

Gregorieff, Dimitry. "Historical Background of Russian Orthodoxy in America," *St. Vladimir's Theological Quarterly,* V, 1-2 (Crestwood, N.Y., 1961), pp. 2-53.

Gulanich, George. *Golden-Silver-Jubilee,* 1896-1921-1946. Uniontown, Pa., 1946.

Gulovich, Stephen C. "Byzantine Slavonic Catholics and the Latin Clergy," *Homiletic and Pastoral Review,* XLV, 7-9 (New York, 1945), pp. 517-527, 586-596, 675-680.

————. "The Rusin Exarchate in the United States," *Eastern Churches Quarterly,* VI (London, 1946), pp. 459-485.

————. *Windows Westward: Rome-Russia-Reunion.* New York: Declan X. McMullen, 1947.

Hardyi, Petro S. *Korotka istoriia Lemkovskoho relifovoho komiteta v SShA: moia podorozh' na Lemkovshchinu.* Yonkers, N.Y.: Lemko Soiuz, 1958.

Hightower, Michael J. "The Road to Russian Hill: A Story of Immigration and Coal Mining," *Chronicles of Oklahoma,* LXIII, 3 (Oklahoma City, 1985), pp. 228-249.

Himka, John-Paul. "Ivan Volians'kyi," *Ukraïns'kyi istoryk,* XII, 3-4 (New York, Toronto, and Munich, 1975), pp. 61-72.

Hutnyan, Andrew, ed. *American Carpatho-Russian Orthodox Greek Catholic Diocese Commemorative Jubliee Journal Fiftieth Golden Anniversary, 1938-1988.* Johnstown, Pa: American Carpatho-Russian Orthodox Greek Catholic Diocese, 1988.

Iubileinyi sbornik v pamiat' 150-lietiia Russkoi pravoslavnoi tserkvi v Sievernoi Amerikie, 2 vols. New York: Iubileinaia komissiia, 1944-45.

Jankura, Stephen. *History of the Russian Orthodox Catholic Mutual Aid Society of the U.S.A.—Diamond Jubilee.* Wilkes Barre, Pa., 1970.

Jurchisin, Mitro. *Carpathian Village People: A Listing of Immigrants to Minneapolis, Minnesota from the 1880s to 1947.* Minneapolis, Minn.: p.a., 1981.

Kirshbaum, Joseph M. *Slovaks in Canada.* Toronto: Canadian Ethnic Press Association of Ontario, 1967, esp. "Slovak Greek Catholic Parishes and Missions," pp. 249-268.

Kohanik, Peter. *Do zahal'noi vîdomosty russkoho naroda v Spoluchennŷkh Derzhavakh.* n.p., 1916.

————. *Iubileinyi sbornik Soiuza pravoslavnykh sviashchennikov v Amerikie.* Passaic, N.J., 1960.

————. *Russkia Pravoslavnaia Tserkov i sovremennoe karpatorusskoe dvizhenie v Sievernoi Amerikie.* Passaic, N.J., 1946.

————. *The Most Useful Knowledge for the RussoAmerican Young People.* Passaic, N.J., 1934.

————. "Nachalo istorii Amerikanskoi Rusi." In Filipp I. Svistun, *Prikarpatskaia Rus' pod vladeniem Avstrii.* 2nd ed. Trumbull, Conn.: Peter S. Hardy, 1970, pp. 467-515.

————. *Rus' i pravoslavie v Sievernoi Amerikie: k XXV lietiiu Russkago pravoslavnago obshchestva vzaimopomoshchi.* Wilkes Barre, Pa.: Russkoe pravoslavnoe kafolicheskoe obshchestvo vzaimopomoshchi, 1920.

————. [Kokhanik, Petr]. *Russkoe pravoslavnoe kafolicheskoe obshchestvo vzaimopomoshchi v sev.-amerikanskikh Soedinennykh Shtatakh: k XX-lietnemu iubileiu 1895-1915.* New York: Russkoe pravoslavnoe kafolicheskoe obshchestvo vzaimopomoshchi, 1915.

————. [Kohanik, Petr Iur'evich]. *[Seventieth] 70th Anniversary: Russkoe Pravoslavnoe obshchestvo vzaimo-pomoshchi v sieverno-amerikanskikh Soedinennykh Shtatakh.* Wilkes-Barre, Pa.: Russkoe pravoslavnoe kafolicheskoe obshchestvo vzaimopomoshchi, 1965.

Kondratovics, Irén. "Az amerikai ruszinok," *Magyar szemle,* XLII, 1 (Budapest, 1942), pp. 21-24.

Konstankevych, I. and Bonchevs'kyi, A. *Uniia v Amerytsi.* New York, 1902.

Kuropas, Myron B. *The Ukrainian Americans: Roots and Aspirations, 1884-1954.* Toronto, Buffalo, and London: University of Toronto Press, 1991.

Lacko, Michael. "The Churches of Eastern Rite in North America," *Unitas,* XVI, 2 (Graymoor/Garrison, N.Y., 1964), pp. 89-115.

Ladižinsky, Ivan A. *Karpatorossy v Europi i Ameriki: primir Kamjonka.* Cleveland: Svet, 1940.

Lesko, David. "Eternal Memory: Bishop Stephen (Dzubay)," *Quarterly Newsletter,* Nos. 3-4 and 1-2 (Wexford, Pa., 1978-79), pp. 4, 4, 4, 3.

Litva, Felix, ed. *Stefan B. Roman: človek v rozdvojenom svete/Man in a Divided World.* Cambridge, Ont.: Friends of Good Books, 1981.

Lowig, Evan. "The Historical Development of Ukrainians within the Orthodox Church in America: A Comparative Study." In David J. Goa. *The Ukrainian Religious Experience: Tradition and the Canadian Cultural Context*. Edmonton, Alta: Canadian Institute of Ukrainian Studies, University of Alberta, 1989, pp. 209-218.

Lukas [Lukáč], Michael. "Pät'desiat rokov vyst'ahovalectva z Karpát do Kanady." In *Vyst'ahovalectvo a život krajanov vo svete: k storočici začiatkov maseveho vyst'ahovalectva slovenského l'udu do zámoria*. Martin: Matica Slovenska, 1982, pp. 303-306.

————. *45 Anniversary, 1929-1974: Society of Carpatho-Russian Canadians*. Toronto, 1974.

————. *50 Anniversary, 1929-1979: Society of Carpatho-Russian Canadians/Obshchestvo karpatorusskykh kanadtsev*. Toronto, [1979].

Lutsyk, Ieronim Ia. [Roman Surmach]. "Istoriia Amerikanskoi Rusi." In idem. *Narodnaia istoriia Rusi ot naidavnieishikh vremen do nynieshnikh dnei*. New York: Ivan Gr. Borukh, 1911, pp. 325-341.

Magocsi, Paul Robert. *The Carpatho-Rusyn Americans*. The Peoples of North America Series. New York and Philadelphia: Chelsea House Publishers, 1989.

————. "The Carpatho-Rusyn Press." In Sally M. Miller, ed. *The Ethnic Press in the United States*. Westport, Conn.: Greenwood Press, 1987, pp. 15-26.

————. "Carpatho-Rusyns." In Dirk Hoerder, ed. *The Immigrant Labor Press in North America, 1840s-1970s: An Annotated Bibliography*, Vol. II. New York, Westport, Conn., and London: Greenwood Press, 1987, pp. 385-400.

————. "Carpatho-Rusyns." In Francesco Cordasco, ed. *Dictionary of American Immigration History*. Metuchen, N.J. and London: Scarecrow Press, 1990, pp. 105-109.

————. "Carpatho-Rusyns." In Stephan Thernstrom, ed. *Harvard Encyclopedia of American Ethnic Groups*. Cambridge, Mass. and London, England: The Belknap Press of Harvard University Press, 1980, pp. 200-210.

————. "Carpatho-Rusyns in Ontario." In Lubomyr Y. Luciuk and Iroida L. Wynnyckyj, eds. *Ukrainians in Ontario/Polyphony*, Vol. X. Toronto: Multicultural History Society of Ontario, 1988, pp. 177-190.

————. "Carpatho-Ruthenian." In *The World's Written Languages: A Survey of the Degree and Modes of Use*, Vol. 1: *The Americas*. Québec: Université Laval, 1978, pp. 553-561.

————. "Immigrants from Eastern Europe: The Carpatho-Rusyn Community of Proctor, Vermont," *Vermont History*, XLII, I (Montpelier, Vt., 1974), pp. 48-52. Reprinted in *Rutland Historical Society Quarterly*, XV, 2 (Rutland, Vt., 1985), pp. 18-23.

————. "Karpato-rusyny u Ameryky," *Nova dumka*, VIII [20] (Vukovar, 1979), pp. 67-73; [21], pp. 97-100; [22], pp. 69-73.

————. "Made or Re-Made in America?: Nationality and Identity Formation Among Carpatho-Rusyn Immigrants and Their Descendants," *Coexistence—Special Issue: The Emigré Experience*, XXVIII (Dordrecht, Netherlands, 1991), pp. 335-348. Also in Paul Robert Magocsi, ed. *The Persistence of Regional Cultures: Rusyns and Ukrainians in Their Homeland and Abroad*. New York: East European Quarterly/Columbia University Press, 1993, pp.

————. "The Political Activity of Rusyn-American Immigrants in 1918," *East European Quarterly*, X, 3 (Boulder, Colo., 1976), pp. 347-365.

————. "Rusyn-American Ethnic Literature." In *Ethnic Literatures Since 1776: The Many Voices of America*, Vol. II. Lubbock, Texas: Texas Tech University, 1978, pp. 503-520.

————. "Rusyn-Americans and Czechoslovakia." In Bohomír Bunža, ed. *Rada Svobodného Československa/Council of Free Czechoslovakia: Historie, program, činnost, dokumenty*. Toronto: Rada Svobodného Československa, 1990, pp. 206-211.

————. "Rusynn-Americans, Slovak-Americans, and Czecho-Slovakia." In Josef Stefka, ed. *Kalendár-Almanac National Slovak Society of the USA for the Year of 1990*. Pittsburgh, Pa., 1990, pp. 59-62.

Mamatey, Victor S. "The Slovaks and Carpatho-Ruthenians." In Joseph P. O'Grady, ed. *The Immigrant's Influence on Wilson's Peace Policies.* Lewisburg, Ky.: University of Kentucky Press, 1967, pp. 224-249.

Masich, John. "Highlights in the Glorious History of the Greek Catholic Union of the U.S.A." In *Jubilee Almanac of the Greek Catholic Union of the U.S.A.*, Vol. LXXI. Munhall, Pa.: Greek Catholic Union, 1967, pp. 33-95 and 258-263.

Matrosov, E.N. "Zaokeanskaia Rus'," *Istoricheskii viestnik*, LXVII, 1-5 (Moscow, 1897), pp. 131, 478, 853, 83, and 435. Reprinted in F. Svistun, *Prikarpatskaia Rus' pod vladeniem Avstrii.* 2nd. ed. Trumbull, Conn.: Peter S. Hardy, 1970, pp. 516-531.

Maynard, Theodore. *The Better Part: The Life of Teresa Demjanovich.* New York: Macmillan, 1952.

Medieshi, Liubomir. "Amerikantsi ruskoho pokhodzenia." In Diura Latiak, ed. *Narodni kalendar 1989.* Novi Sad: Ruske slovo, 1988, pp. 91-100.

————. "Ameritski Karpatoruski Vyhliedovatski Tsentr." In Diura Latiak, ed. *Narodni kalendar 1990.* Novi Sad: Ruske slovo, 1989, pp. 191-196.

————. "Ameritski Rusnatsi prez svoiu presu," *Shvetlosts*, XXVI, 2 (Novi Sad, 1988), pp. 199-225.

————. "'Podkorman'oshe'—putniki tvardei nadiï." In Diura Latiak, ed. *Narodni kalendar 1988.* Novi Sad: Ruske slovo, 1987, pp. 71-83.

————. "Rodoliubivi pisnï iuhoslavianskikh Rusnatsokh obiaveni u Ameriki," *Shvetlosts*, XXV, 5 (Novi Sad, 1987), pp. 691-705.

Michaylo, George. *Official Anniversary Volume 1902-1942: Forty Years in the Priesthood of his Excellency Basil Takach.* McKeesport: Prosvita, 1942.

Miliasevich, Iona. *Kratii istoricheskii ocherk zhizni Russkago pravoslavnago zhenskago obshchestva vzaimopomoshchi v S.Sh.S.A. so dnia osnovaniia obshchestva l-go iulia 1907 g. po l-e marta 1926 goda.* Coaldale, Pa., 1926.

Mushynka, Mykola. "Do 100-richchia z dnia narodzhennia ta 20-richchia z dnia smerti Dmytra Vyslots'koho/Vania Hunianky." In *Repertuarnyi zbirnyk*, No. 2. Prešov: Kul'turnyi soiuz ukraïns'kykh trudiashchykh, 1989.

————. "Emilii Kubek—pershyi romanist Zakarpattia." In *Ukraïns'kyi kalendar 1980.* Warsaw, 1980, pp. 213-215.

Mytsiuk, Oleksander. "Z emihratsiï uhro-rusyniv pered svitovoiu viinoiu," *Naukovyi zbirnyk tovarystva 'Prosvita', XIII-XIV* (Uzhhorod, 1937-38) pp. 21-32.

"The New Republic of Rusinia, Mostly Made in America," *Literary Digest*, LXIX, 13 (New York, 1921), pp. 41-43.

Obushkevich, Feofan. *Ustroistvo russkikh gr. kaf. gromad tserkovnykh v Soed. Shtatakh Ameriki.* New York: Pravda, 1906.

Ol., M. "Deshcho z istoriï uhro-ruskoï parokhiï v Lethbridge, Alta." In *Iliustrovanyi kalendar kanads'koho ukraïntsia na rik 1925.* Winnipeg, 1924, pp. 93-94.

"Osnovanie Russkago Narodnago Soiuza, Russkago Pravoslavnago Obshchestva Vzaimopomoshchi i Obshchestva Russkikh Bratstv." In Filip Svistun, *Prikarpatskaia Rus' pod vladeniem Avstrii.* 2nd ed. Trumbull, Conn.: Peter S. Hardy, 1970, pp. 497-514.

Padokh, Iaroslav. "Emigratsiia." In Bohdan O. Strumins'kyi, ed. *Lemkivshchyna*, Vol. II. Zapysky Naukovoho tovarystva im. Shevchenka, Vol. 206. New York, Paris, Sydney, and Toronto, 1988, pp. 463-484.

Palij, Michael. "Early Ukrainian Immigration to the United States and the Conversion of the Ukrainian Catholic Parish in Minneapolis to Russian Orthodoxy," *Journal of Ukrainian Studies,* VIII, 2 (Toronto, 1983), pp. 13-37.

Pamiatka k 20-lietiiu arkhiereiskago sluzheniia Arkhiepiskopa Lavra/An Album Commemorating the Twentieth Year of Hierarchical Service of Archbishop Laurus. [Jordanville, N.Y., 1987].

Pamiatkova kniha z nahody toržestvennaho posvjaščenija maternaho monastyra Sester Čina Sv. Vasilija Velikoho na Hori Sv. Makriny vo Uniontown, Penna. McKeesport, Pa.: Prosvita-Enlightenment, 1934.

Pamiatna knyzhka 10-lityia Lemko-Soiuza v Soed. Shtatakh y Kanadi y otkrŷtyia Karpatorusskoho amerykanskoho tsentra maia 28, 1939. [Yonkers, N.Y.: Lemko Soiuz, 1939].

Papp, A. "Korotkij perehlad istoriji Sobranija za 1903-1928 rr." In *Kalendar Sobranija na r. 1926.* McKeesport, Pa., 1929, pp. 136-152.

Pekar, Athanasius B. "Historical Background of the Carpatho-Ruthenians in America," *Ukraïns'kyi istoryk,* XIII, 1-4 (New York, Toronto, and Munich, 1976), pp. 87-102 and XIV, 1-2 (1977), pp. 70-84.

————. *Our Past and Present: Historical Outlines of the Byzantine Ruthenian Metropolitan Province.* Pittsburgh, Pa.: Byzantine Seminary Press, 1974.

————. "Sheptyts'kyi and the Carpatho-Ruthenians in the United States." In Paul Robert Magocsi, ed. *Morality and Reality: the Life and Times of Andrei Sheptyts'kyi.* Edmonton: University of Alberta Canadian Institute of Ukrainian Studies, 1989, pp. 363-374.

Pel'ts, Stepan A. "Do istoriï lemkivs'koï emigratsiï v ZDA." In *Lemkivs'kyi kalendar na 1965 rik.* Torotno and Pasaic, N.J.: Orhanizatsiia Oborony Lemkivshchyny, 1965, pp. 47-61.

Pospishil, Victor J. *Compulsory Celibacy for the Eastern Catholics in the Americas.* Toronto: Church of St. Demetrius Ukrainian Catholic Women's League, 1977.

Pravda ob ukrayntsiakh. Mahanoy City, Pa., 1903.

Procko, Bohdan P. "The Establishment of the Ruthenian Church in the United States, 1884-1907," *Pennsylvania History,* XLII, 2 (Bloomsburg, Pa., 1975), pp. 137-154.

————. "Soter Ortynsky: First Ruthenian Bishop in the United States, 1907-1916," *Catholic Historical Review,* LVIII, 4 (Washington, D.C., 1973), pp. 513-533.

Ramach, Liubomir. "Rusnatsi u Kanadi." *Khristiianskii kalendar za 1972 rok.* Ruski Krstur, 1972, pp. 106-110.

Renoff, Richard. "Carpatho-Ruthenian Resources and Assimilation, 1880-1924," *Review Journal of Philosophy and Social Science*, II, 1 (Meerut, India, 1977), pp. 53-78.

————. "Community and Nationalism in the Carpatho-Russian Celibacy Schism: Some Sociological Hypotheses," *Diakonia*, VI, 1 (New York, 1971), pp. 58-68.

Renoff, Richard and Reynolds, Stephen, eds. *Proceedings of the Conference on Carpatho-Ruthenian Immigration, 8 June 1974.* Cambridge, Mass.: Harvard Ukrainian Research Institute Sources and Documents Series, 1975.

Roman, Jaroslav. "The Establishment of the American Carpatho-Russian Orthodox Greek Catholic Diocese in 1938: A Major Carpatho-Russian Return to Orthodoxy," *St. Vladimir's Theological Quarterly,* XX, 3 (Crestwood/Tuckahoe, N.Y., 1976), pp. 132-160.

Roman, Michael. "Istorija Greko-Kaft. Sojedinenija." In *Zoloto-Jubilejnyj Kalendar' Greko Kaft. Sojedinenija v S.Š.A.,* XLVII. Munhall, Pa.: Greko Kaftoličeskoje Sojedinenije, 1942, pp. 39-74.

Russin, Keith S. "Father Alexis G. Toth and the Wilkes-Barre Litigations," *St. Vladimir's Theological Quarterly*, XVI, 3 (Tuckahoe, N.Y., 1972), pp. 123-149.

Samielo, Roman N. "Amerikanskii Russkii Karpatorusskii Soiuz o sud'bie Lemkoviny Priashevshchiny i Kholmshchiny." In I. Gr. Dzvonchik, comp. *Iubileinyi al'manakh 1900-1950.* Philadelphia, Pa.: Obshchestvo Russkikh Bratstv, [1950], pp. 161-170.

Schmal, Desmond A. "The Ruthenian Question," *American Ecclesiastical Review,* XCVII (Washington, D.C., 1937), pp. 448-461.

Seniuk, D. O. *Mitrofornyi protoierei Andrei Stepanovich Shlepetskii: kratkii ocherk zhizni i deiatel'nosti.* Prešov, 1967.

Serafim (Surrency), Archimandrite. *The Quest for Orthodox Church Unity in America.* New York: Boris and Gleb Press, 1973.

Shereghy, Basil. *Bishop Basil Takach 'The Good Shepherd'.* Pittsburgh, Pa., 1979.

————. *Fifty Years of Piety: A History of the Uniontown Pilgrimages.* Pittsburgh, Pa.: Byzantine Seminary Press, 1985.

————. ed. *The United Societies of the U.S.A.: A Historical Album.* McKeesport, Pa., 1978.

Shipman, Andrew J. "Greek Catholics in America." In *The Catholic Encyclopedia*, Vol. VI. New York: The Gilmary Society, 1913, pp. 744-750.

Shlepetskii, Aleksander S. "Karpatorossi v Ameriki." In *Almanakh O.K.S. Vozrozhdenie*. Prague, 1936, pp. 81-86.

———. "Priashevtsi v Amerike." In Ivan S. Shlepetskii, ed. *Priashevshchina: istoriko-literaturnyi sbornik*. Prague: Khutor, 1948, pp. 255-262.

Simirenko, Alex. "The Minneapolis Russian Community in Transition," *St. Vladimir's Seminary Quarterly*, V, 1-2 (Crestwood/Tuckahoe, N.Y., 1961), pp. 88-100.

———. *Pilgrims, Colonists, and Frontiersmen: An Ethnic Community in Transition.* New York: Free Press of Glencoe, 1964.

———. "The Social Structure of the Minneapolis Russian Community." In *Proceedings of the Minnesota Academy of Science for 1959.* Minneapolis, 1959, pp. 79-86.

Sister of Charity [M. Zita]. *Sister Miriam Teresa (1901-1927).* Convent Station, N.J.: Sister Miriam Teresa League of Prayer, 1936.

Stein, Howard F. "An Ethnohistory of Slovak-American Religious and Fraternal Associations: A Study in Cultural Meaning, Group Identity, and Social Institutions," *Slovakia*, XXIX (West Paterson, N.J., 1980-81), pp. 53-101.

Stryps'kyi, Hiiador. "Uhors'ki rusyny i slovaky v Amerytsi," *Zhytie i slovo*, VI (L'viv, 1897), pp. 414-420.

Tajtak, Ladislav. "Pereselennia ukraïntsiv Skhidnoï Slovachchyny do 1913 r.," *Duklia*, IX, 4 (Prešov, 1961), pp. 97-103.

———. "Východoslovenské výsťahovalectvo do prvej svetovej vojny," *Nové obzory*, III (Prešov, 1961), pp. 221-247.

Tarasar, Constance J. and Erickson, John H. eds. *Orthodox America, 1794-1976: Development of the Orthodox Church in America.* Syosset, N.Y., 1975.

Tverdyi Rusyn [0. Stetkevych]. *Bery y chytai.* New York: Svoboda, 1908.

Turkevich, V. *Pravoslavnoe obshchestvo vzaimopomoshchi v sievero-amerikanskikh Soedinennykh Shtatakh: k X-lietnemu iuvileiu, 1895-1905.* Bridgeport, Conn.: Pravoslavnoe obshchestvo vzaimo-pomoshchi, 1905.

Vostok—The East: Twenty-Fifth Anniversary, 1918-1943. Perth Amboy, N.J., 1945.

Vyslotskyi, D.F., ed. *Nasha knyzhka.* Yonkers: Lemko-Soiuz v ShSA y Kanadi, 1945.

Winslow, B. "Catholics of the Byzantine Rite," *Eastern Churches Quarterly*, V (London, 1944), pp. 319-324.

Warzeski, Walter C. *Byzantine Rite Rusins in Carpatho-Ruthenia and America.* Pittsburgh, Pa.: Byzantine Seminary Press, 1971.

———. "The Rusin Community in Pennsylvania." In John Bodnar, ed. *The Ethnic Experience in Pennsylvania.* Lewisburg, Pa.: Bucknell University Press, 1973, pp. 175-215.

Yurčišin, Joan. *Korotka cerkovna istorija karpatorusskaho naroda.* Johnstown, Pa.: Amerikanska Karpatorusska Pravoslavna Greko Kaftoličeskaja Jeparchija, 1954.

Zatkovich, Gregory. *The Tragic Tale.* Pittsburgh, Pa., 1926.

Zhirosh, Miron. "Odkhod nashikh liudzokh do Kanadi i Argentini (u shvetlie 'Ruskikh novinokh', 1924-1933)." In Diura Latiak, ed. *Narodni kalendar 1984.* Novi Sad: Ruske slovo, 1983, pp. 46-59.

———. "Rusnak—ameritski men." In Iuliian Kamenitski, ed. *Ruski kalendar 1994.* Novi Sad: Ruske slovo, 1994, pp. 29-35.

Zięba, Andrzej. "Poland and Political Life in Carpatho-Rus and Among Carpatho-Rusyns in Emigration and North America, 1918-1939." In Paul J. Best, ed. *Contributions of the Carpatho-Rusyn Studies Group to the IV World Congress for Soviet and East European Studies.* New Haven, Conn.: Carpatho-Rusyn Studies Group, 1990, pp. 23-39.

Zsatkovics, Kalman. *Rules for the Spiritual Government of Greek-Ruthenian Catholics in the United States.* New York, n.d.

Index

Public charities, *see* Socioeconomic status
Publishers and booksellers, 81. *See also* Culture;
    Newspapers, journals and pamphlets
Pysh, Simeon (1894-1968), 61 (and illus.), 82, 91

Quebec, 104

Rachiv, 7
Racine, William, 57
Rada club, 110
Rada Svobodnoj Podkarpatskoj Rusi v Exili, *see* Council
    of a Free Sub-Carpathia-Ruthenia in Exile
Radio Free Europe, 108
Radio programs, *see* Culture
Rahway, New Jersey, 19
Railroad(s): in Subcarpathian Rus', 12, 13; U. S., Carpa-
    tho-Rusyn workers on, 21
Ratica, Peter (1883-196?), 91
Reagan, Ronald, 86
Red Army, 91, 107. *See also* Russia/Soviet Union
Red Cross, 107
Red Scare (1950s), 41. *See also* Communist
    party/Communism
Regionalism, *see* Nationalism
Relief organizations (public charities), *see* Socioeconomic
    status
Religion: and anticlericalism, 62; and architecture, *see*
    Church architecture; and church membership, *see*
    Demographic statistics; and church music, 70 (*see also*
    Culture); and church property, *see* Land ownership;
    and community life, 25; as cultural identifier, 10,
    11-12, 25, 65, 66 (illus.), 67-68 (and illus.), 98, (vs.
    confusion over identity) 62 (*see also* Ethnic/national
    identity); dissension in, 27, 29-31, 33, 35, 37-43, 98;
    fraternal organizations and church affairs, *see* Fraternal
    organizations; and inner city churches, 22; and
    missionary efforts, 30, 46; and nationalism, 11, 31, 95,
    98; and religious affiliation in U.S., 34 (chart); and
    religious jurisdiction, 30, 31, 35-44 passim, 95; and
    religious life in U.S., 25-47; and religious retreats
    (*otpusti*), 72, 73, 74 (illus.). *See also* Byzantine
    (Eastern) rites; Byzantine Ruthenian Catholic Church;
    Catholic Church; Celibacy issue; Convent(s); Culture;
    Eastern Christianity; Latin rites; Monastery(ies);
    Orthodoxy-Protestantism; Roman Catholic Church;
    Ukrainian Catholic Church
Renoff, Richard (b. 1936), 3, 82
Repa, Ivan, 51
Republican party, 85. *See also* Politics
Research centers, *see* Culture
Reshetar, John (b. 1924), 82
Retreats, *see* Religion
Revay, Julian (1899-1979), 60 (and illus.), 91
Revolution of 1989, 4
Righetti, John, 4
Rijeka, Yugoslavia, 14

Robitnyčo-Osvit'ne Karpats'ke Tovarystvo, 106
Rockefeller Park (Cleveland), 57, 59 (illus.)
Rock Springs, Wyoming, 21
Rodez (Ruzzi), France, 9
Rodina, 57
Roman, Jaroslav, 4
Roman, Michael (b. 1912), 3, 56, 82, 95
Roman, Stephen B. (1921-1988), 24, 105 (and illus.)
Roman Catholic Church: attitude of, toward Greek
    Catholic Church, *see* Byzantine Ruthenian Catholic
    Church; conversion to, 37, 45-46; excommunication
    from, 39, 55; fraternal organizations of, 49; Greek
    Catholicism distinguished from, 11; in Hungary and
    Poland, 11; influence of, 8, 11; union with, 11,
    (abrogation of) 40, (vs. east-west division) 9, (vs.
    Greek Catholic) 25, 27, 29-30
Romania: emigration via, 14; villages of, 7, 106, 111
Ros, *see* Carpatho-Rusyn people
Rosocha, Stepan (1908-1986), 109, 110
Rostropovich, Mystyslav, 47
Roswell, Georgia, 68, 72 (illus.)
Royalton, Illinois, 21
Royster, Bishop Dmitri, 34 (chart)
Rozhdestvensky, Archbishop Platon (1866-1934), 30-33,
    35-37
Rus', 9-11, 105
Rusin (as term), *see* Carpatho-Rusyn people
Rusin/Ruthenian, 92, 108
Rusin/The Ruthenian, 53 (illus.), 54
Rusin Association of Minnesota, 60
Rusin Council for National Defense (1922), 90
Rusin Cultural Garden (Cleveland), 57-58, 59 (illus.)
Rusin Day Association of Greater Cleveland, 57. *See also*
    Rusyn Day
Rusin Educational Society, 57
Rusin Elite Society, 57
Rusinko, Elaine (b. 1949), 82
Ruska dolina (Rusyn valley) of Pittsburgh, 83. *See also*
    Pittsburgh, Pennsylvania
Ruska Matka, 102
Rus'ka skola (Rusyn school), 78. *See also* Schools
Ruski Kerestur, Yugoslavia, 102, 110
Rusnak, Bishop Michael (b. 1921), 105
Rusnak/Russniak (as term), *see* Carpatho-Rusyn people
Russia/Russian Empire, 36, 86, 106; emigration from, 86;
    church in, 36; and pro-Russian nationalism, 56, 58, 60
    (*see also* Russophiles); Soviet Russia, 36, 91; tsarist
    Russia, and Orthodox movement, 30, 31, 86; unifica-
    tion of Carpatho-Rusyn lands with, 86, 105, 106
Russian Bank (Mukačevo), 93, 94 (illus.)
"Russian" churches, 1. *See also* Byzantine Ruthenian
    Catholic Church; Church architecture
Russian Brotherhood Organization (Obščestvo Russkich
    Bratstv), 51
Russian Messenger, see Russkij vistnik
Russian National Brotherhood, *see* American Russian

Photo Credits

The author and publisher wish to thank the following individuals, institutions, and publishers for supplying photographs and/or granting permission to reproduce them from existing publications. Their courtesy is gratefully acknowledged:

Connie Zatkovich Ash, Cornwall, Oregon—85; Peter Baycura, Butler, Pa.—54, 58; Byzantine Ruthenian Catholic Archdiocese of Pittsburgh—25, 26, 65, 93; Carpatho-Rusyn Research Center, Fairview, N.J.—77; Center for Research Libraries, Chicago—82; Chelsea House Publishers, Philadelphia, Pa.—92; Cleveland Cultural Garden Federation—44; Greek Catholic Congregation of St. John the Baptist, Perth Amboy, N.J.—72, 74; Greek Catholic Union, Beaver, Pa.—17, 24, 34, 36, 38, 39, 40, 49, 50, 63, 66, 96; Heritage Institute, Byzantine Ruthenian Catholic Diocese of Passaic—1, 2, 3, 8, 10, 11, 12, 16, 19, 35, 42, 55, 83, 87; Roman S. Holiat, Riverdale, N.Y.—45; Immigration History Research Center, St. Paul, Minn.—37, 43, 73, 76; Jerry Jumba, McKees Rocks, Pa.—67, 90; Paul Kobelak, Cleveland—48; Lemko Association, Yonkers, N.Y.—46, 47; Ljubomir Medješi, Novi Sad, Yugoslavia—101; Orestes Mihaly, Armonk, N.Y.—15, 23, 56, 62; Orthodox Church in America Archives, Syosset, N.Y.—18, 30, 53; Osvĕta Publishers, Martin, Slovakia—51; Pennsylvania Historical and Museum Commission, Harrisburg—6; Princeton University Press, Princeton, N.J.—84; John Righetti, Pittsburgh, Pa.—64; Chetko Collection, Roberson Center for the Arts and Sciences, Binghamton, N.Y.—7; St. Mary's Catholic Church of the Byzantine Rite, New York City—60; St. Mary's Orthodox Church, Minneapolis, Minn.—13, 14; John Schweich, Minneapolis—9; the Reverend Philip P. Scott, Roswell, Ga.—61; Society of Carpatho-Russian Canadians, Toronto—98, 99, 100; Universal-International Pictures, New York City—78; University of Chicago Press—57; Vostok Publishing Co., Perth Amboy, N.J.—91; Worldwide Church of God, Pasadena, Ca.—32; Msgr. John Yurcisin, Johnstown, Pa.—20, 21 22, 27, 28, 41, 59; Anton Žižka, Prešov, Slovakia—52; Alexander Zozul'ák, Prešov, Slovakia—94, 95.